Studies in Spanish Phonology

MIAMI LINGUISTICS SERIES

No. 1. Germanic Studies in Honor of Edward Henry Sehrt
*Edited by Frithjof A. Raven, Wolfram K. Legner,
and James C. King*

No. 2. A Linguistic Study of the English Verb
By F. R. Palmer

No. 3. A Multilingual Lexicon of Linguistics and Philology:
English, Russian, German, French
Compiled by Rose Nash

Miami Linguistics Series No. 4

Studies in
Spanish Phonology

By TOMÁS NAVARRO

Translated by
RICHARD D. ABRAHAM

UNIVERSITY OF MIAMI PRESS
Coral Gables, Florida

Contents

Preface

THE STUDIES GATHERED in this book refer for their greatest part to those traits of Spanish phonology more directly related to the oral aspect of the language. Some of these studies are essays that have been taken from previous works and then revised. All have been intended as a contribution toward the knowledge of the characteristics that form the peculiar sound image that gives Spanish its distinctive physiognomy among the other languages. Their publication in English now offers an opportunity for adding this preface as well as for including an old note on the unfoldment of vocalic phonemes in Andalusian dialect.

It is a known fact that every phoneme, together with its ideologic function, constitutes an acoustic symbol of variable phonetic effect. The majority of the Spanish phonemes are present too in the other European languages. In fact, there is not a single one that fails to appear also in at least one other language. Nevertheless, the oral impression that characterizes Spanish is not the natural result of the significance of the phonemes as abstract phonic types, but rather of the relative proportion of their total scale of frequency and of the special circumstances of the sounds with which they are normally produced.

It should be kept in mind that the ideologic and voiced abstraction of the phoneme leaves out a number of elements quite significant within the expressive spectrum of the spoken word. Among such elements we have the articulatory modifications and variants that tell the locality or region where an individual is from, the social class he belongs to, his cultural and educational level, the quality of his manners and behavior, and the occasional state of his emotional temper. These vital semantic elements of a social nature, and not merely the acoustic-physiological analysis of sounds, constitute the true field of modern phonetics.

There is no question that the main factor in the phonic characterization of Spanish lies in the firmness, simplicity, and clarity of its vowels. The causes that have influenced this language during the development of such a vocalic system remain yet unknown. Something that stands out with suggestive significance is the striking resemblance of the Spanish vowels, in articulation and timbre and in the simplicity of their phonological totality, to the ones of the prehistoric Basque tongue, the geographical neighbor of Spanish in the Peninsula. Even though they are not, of course, perfectly identical, it becomes quite obvious that the vocalic sounds of Spanish are considerably nearer to those of Basque than to those of Catalan or Portuguese—notwithstanding the common Romanic origin of the latter two with Spanish.

The simplicity of the Spanish vocalic series contrasts with the notorious profusion of its fourteen dipthongs. The notion of the phonemic unity of the diphthong, paradoxically denied by some phonologists against its general acceptance by phoneticians, is based on the idea of its etymological tradition and, above all, on the constant and vital example of verbal flexion. In the linguistic experience of every person, the diphthong *ie* and the vowels *e, i* behave with an analogous phonemic value in *siento, sentimos, sintamos*. The incidental phonetic relation between the first element of the diphthong *ie* and the vowel *i* constitutes no reason, even with the support of orthography, for the presence, more or less modified, of this vowel in the body of the diphthong to be noticed. Likewise, the morphological link between *puedo, podemos, pudimos* puts the phonemes *ue, o, u* on a same level, without any suggestion whatever that *ue* is to be seen as the sum of two distinct phonemes. The phonemic equivalence between diphthongs and vowels can be observed also in contrasting pairs such as *baila–bala, causa–casa, peina–pena, pauta–pata.* There is no indication that will cause the second elements of these authentic diphthongs to be perceived as reduced vowels. The same may be said of the initial elements of the diphthongs *ie, ue* in contrasts such as *tierno–terno, mienta–menta, muesca–mosca, duende–donde.* The case is different with occasional diphthongs formed by synalepha. In these the double composition of the phoneme remains latent: *letra–impresa, noche–inquieta, fuerza–unida,* etc.

In the intricate correlation of the phonic units that form the oral structure of the language, the basic correspondence of the melodic groups with the metric types of versification must be taken into account. Within the ordinary fluctuation of such groups, in what concerns their syllabic extension, it is a proven fact that the measure of eight syllables is the most current in standard Spanish elocution. It is not venturesome to assume that this phonologic habit has contributed to the development of the octosyllable as a form perpetually predominant in Spanish poetry. But it must be realized also that the octosyllable, like other Spanish verses, does not present, outside of its syllabic measure, a definite and constant form. On the contrary, in the manner of the phoneme and the toneme, it is composed under various rhythmic modalities, each having a certain expressive value of its own. I discussed this question also in "El octosílabo y sus modalidades," *Estudios hispánicos,* in honor of Archer M. Huntington, Wellesley, Mass., 1952, pp. 435–455, and in *Métrica española,* New York, N.Y., 1956, pp. 45–50.

These questions will receive further consideration in the following chapters. I shall add here another visible correlation between the five vocalic phonemes and the five basic tonemes of Spanish intonation. There is an evident parallelism between the gradual scale of the timbre of the vowels and that of the musical height of the tonemes. Medial vowel *a*—medial suspension toneme; low vowel *u*—low cadence toneme; high vowel *i*—high anticadence toneme; semilow vowel *o*—semilow semicadence toneme; semihigh vowel *e*—semihigh semianticadence toneme. Vowels and tonemes are different in their nature and function; in number and proportion they are equivalent. Determining the cause of this correlation or its effects on the structural background of the language is not easy. But, on the other hand, it does not seem correct to attribute the fact to mere and casual coincidence. The intermedial, semilow, and semihigh types of one series play their role by the capital, medial, high, and low types of the other.

Phonological Units

I.

Sounds and Phonemes

In the language of grammar the term phoneme has been used at times to designate any articulated sound. In the use that modern phonology makes of this word, the value attributed to it corresponds to the abstract concept of the sound as a phonetic and semantic unity. The definition of the phoneme has been discussed ever since this word was used in its new sense by the Polish philologist, Baudoin de Courtenay, in 1894. Aside from discrepancies of detail, opinions coincide as to the typical and essential character of the phoneme, as opposed to the particular reality that the sound displays in each of its manifestations.[1]

From the phonetic point of view the pronunciation of a vowel or consonant can undergo articulatory modifications that do not affect the meaning of the word in which the sound occurs. Sounds corresponding to the same linguistic unit offer frequently considerable differences when observed minutely or seen through the apparatus used in such studies. By providing the analysis of these variants, experimental study, which has brought so much progress to our knowledge of the phonetic mechanism of the word, has also made indispensable the consideration of the quality and importance of all the data resulting from such investigations.

When two sounds can alternate in the same word without producing a perceptible effect on the meaning by which that word is known, these sounds, according to the phonological doctrine defined by N. S. Trubetzkoy, are only modifications of the same phoneme. On the other hand, two sounds are different phonemes if they cannot be mutually substituted without affecting the meaning of the word in which they are found. The effect of phonetic changes on the semantic value of words is, therefore, the essential basis that differentiates between sounds and phonemes. The changes of articulation and sonority that the *n*, for example, undergoes in *confuso*, *encima*, and *cinco*, are sounds of the same phoneme. The *y* of *mayo*, with voiced pronunciation, affricate or vibrative, likewise constitutes a single phonological unit. The *r* and the *rr* are, on the other hand, distinct phonemes: *pero–perro*, *caro–carro*.[2]

The same phonemes appear in very different forms. In truth, there is no phoneme that is heard in the same way from all lips. Just as the phoneme represents the ideological type that gives unity to the variety of sounds, the sound itself provides real and concrete form for the theoretical image of the phoneme. The semantic strength of the sound resides in the bond of its phonological affiliation, although its shape may intertwine and multiply in the apparently indivisible chain of articulation. The complete idea of the phoneme unites the essential characteristics of the oral sound in its organic, acoustic, and semantic constitution.[3]

Some phonemes are of universal extent; others are found only in certain languages. Phonemes of a general character do not appear in the same proportion in all languages. The sound image of a language depends greatly on the proportion it uses the phonemes with and specially on the particular modality it follows within the number of variants that such units permit. In describing the oral shapes of the word, it is difficult to establish precise boundaries between sound and phoneme, between phonetics and phonology. At any rate, the general appearance of sounds, the effects produced by their combinations, and, specially, the role they play in relation to the meaning of words are all part of phonology.[4]

Needless to say the consideration the phonological aspect of language demands does not subtract interest from phonetic studies. These are actually indispensable for observing changes in words, for understanding the tendencies that influence the evolution of language, for comparing dialects, and for determining zones and areas of linguistic geography. Even from the point of view of meaning, the ideological value that phonology considers an essential function of the phoneme is far from representing all the expressive activity the variants of the sounds develop according to the subject, occasion, and circumstances in which they are produced.

The phonological and the phonetic systems constitute, furthermore, two different planes in the representation of the spoken word. A unanimous consciousness in a linguistic community is, with respect to the form and value of its phonological elements, the principal basis of the unity of the language. The peculiarities of pronunciation, so often the pride of regional feeling, generally lack significant value in the ambit more consistent and extensive of the phonological system. Actually, regional modalities as well as literary or standard pronunciation, whose forms show more similarities, respond to the coincidental qualification of these abstract and essential units developed through a long and common tradition.

Not always, in the constant evolution of language, has the phonological system been the same, neither do all the units that constitute it appear with equally defined traits. It is not easy to decide to what limits the variants of a phoneme can carry their changes without impairing the shape and function of the type they represent. Personal acquaintance with the distinctions and contrasts between different regions facilitates the identification of such modifications. On the other hand, the total image of the word serves as an aid in the recognition of the phonemes it is made up of, even if they present a variety of forms.

As everyone knows, there are important differences in the pronunciation of the syllable-final *s* in Spanish, depending on the circumstances in which this sound occurs and the class and character of the people who articulate it. There are some other articulatory changes that in certain cases cause the pronunciation to go beyond the limits permitted to its variants. It is true that, even in these cases, one may say, for example, something like *bojque* or *bokque* instead of *bosque* without impending the understanding of this word. But he who pronounces or hears such variants is perfectly aware that the original s has been substituted here by sounds associated more properly with other phonological types. In general, the unity of the word is more resistant than that of the phoneme, although the transfer of phonemes may occasionally have a direct effect on the meaning of the words.

The phonological series of Spanish consists of forty-two phonemes. The number of variants or sounds that these phonemes present in the pronunciation of all the countries where this language is spoken is incalculable. Just in the phonetic inventory of the orthoëpy predominant among educated people, the five phonemes of the vowels amount to twenty distinct variants. The consonant phonemes, nineteen all told, represent more than thirty sounds, not counting dialectal modifications. To this, one has to add six falling diphthongs, eight rising diphthongs, and four triphthongs. From the phonetic point of view, diphthongs and triphthongs can be broken down into vowels, semivowels, and semiconsonants. Phonologically, they have the same function as simple phonemes. What makes celo and cielo or vente and veinte different is not the presence or absence of the i but the total contrast between vowels and diphthongs. Neither is it the impression of one part of the diphthong ue but its entire effect that makes a word like tuerca, for example, different from terca or turca.

Semivowels and semiconsonants do not appear in words with the definite individuality that allows all the other sounds to appear in an isolated intervocalic or interconsonantal position. The feeling of the unity of the diphthong is confirmed by the correspondence of words like puerta–portero, tiene–tenía. The division of the diphthong into independent phonemes would in most cases distort the phonological representation of the word. The idea of such a division can be supported at best by the concurrence of vocalic clusters which in reality are not consolidated diphthongs: trai–trae, pior–peor. The more common diphthongs, ie, ue, come from a unitary base and never seem to have wavered in this phonological tradition.

II.

Frequency of Spanish Phonemes

IN THE TRADITION of grammar it is usual to present sounds with special concentration on the circumstances of their articulation. It is not customary to take into account the volume represented by each phoneme in the totality of the voiced material the language uses. While some phonemes appear only from time to time, others are repeated constantly. The most common ones are, of course, those which contribute most to determine the phonetic character of the respective language, although that character, as has already been pointed out, depends less on the phonemes themselves than on the sounds they are expressed with. The clarity and sonority of phonemes can vary a great deal from one language to another, though their frequency may present similar proportions. The rate of frequency of phonemes is an indispensable norm for knowing the composition of each language, for comparing some languages with others, and for indicating the appropriate order in the teaching of pronunciation.

The following data come from counts made from passages in novels, magazines, and newspapers representing the most common and extensive type of written Spanish. Among these texts, with some 1,500 phonemes each and totaling approximately 20,000, few differences were found. More noticeable discrepancies will probably emerge when these figures are compared with those resulting from an analysis of the spoken language or of literary texts of a more personal style.[1]

According to their degree of frequency, Spanish phonemes form the four following groups.

The group of greatest frequency is that constituted by the vowels *a, e, o* and by the consonant *s*. These four phonemes by themselves alone represent more than 40% of the phonetic material used in any text written in Spanish.

A. The *a* occupies first place in the Spanish phonological series. Its proportion is 13%. The middle type *a, padre, tapa*, predominates to an extraordinary degree; the velar variant of *bajo, baúl*, etc., hardly represents 0.5% within the above figure. In Portuguese, the *a* figures as the first phoneme of the language, but from the viewpoint of acoustic effect, the Portuguese *a* lacks in many cases the clarity and sonority of the Spanish *a*. This vowel does not usually occupy in all languages as predominant a place as in Spanish and Portuguese. In Latin it occupied fourth place, in much lower proportion than the *i* and the *e*. It is not the most abundant phoneme in French, Italian, English, or German either.

E. The *e*, which in Spanish occupies the second place with 11.75%, is with its diverse qualitative modalities the most abundant sound in most European languages. In French, English, and German it reaches proportions above 15%. In Portuguese, on the other hand, it shows the relatively low level of 7.32%. The open variant of this vowel, *guerra, cerca*, represented by 1.37% of the total mentioned, does not have the amplitude, the frequency, or the significative function in Spanish that it has in French, Italian, and other languages. Although the proportion of the *e* competes in some Spanish texts with that of the *a*, the effect of the *e* is notably diminished by the secondary character of the particles that constitute the basis of its abundance: *de, se, que, le*, etc.

O. The *o* occupies third place in the Spanish phonological system, with a proportion of 8.90%. The open variant, *torre, bolsa*, represents somewhat more than 3%. The open variant of the *o* is more abundant than that of the *e*. In Italian the *o* and the *a* counter-balance their phonetic effects around the dominant sound of the *e*. This equality does not exist in French, where the *o* goes down to fifth place with a proportion of 5%, while the *a*, with 12.5%, appears in second place of the series immediately after the *e*. In Portuguese, the grapheme *o* is frequently pronounced as a *u*. The *o* with its proper sound is found in Portuguese to a relatively low degree, namely, 3.50%.

S. Before the vowels *i*, *u*, and before any other consonant, comes the *s* in Spanish with a mean proportion of 8.50%. This figure includes in approximately equal parts syllable-initial *s* and final *s*. The voiced variant of this phoneme, *esbelto*, represents 1% of that figure. The *s* has a relatively high level in French as well as in Portuguese, with proportions similar to Latin of between 6 and 7%. The phonic prominence of the *s* does not consist only of its frequency but of the sibilant and sharp effect of its articulation. In Italian, where the plural is not formed with *s*, the proportion of this sound is below 4%.

The high figure that the *s* reaches in Castilian is further augmented in Andalusian and Spanish-American pronunciation with the share corresponding to the *z* and to the *c* of *ce*, *ci*. With the increase from the *seseo*,* the *s* reaches a proportion in Andalusia and Spanish America that elevates it to third place in the scale, ahead of the *o*. Bello noted the imbalance this development of the *s* brings about in the phonological harmony of the language. English, considered a sibilant language, uses the *s* in a proportion approximately half of that which this sound attains in Spanish.[2]

There comes then a group of sounds whose quality has also a marked influence on the phonological physiognomy of Spanish. They are all, with the exception of the *t*, completely voiced phonemes: *n*, *r*, *l*, *d*, *t*, *i*. They figure individually, with proportions between 4 and 6%, and they represent in toto about a fourth of the phonetic material of the language.

N. Average proportion, 6.94%. The syllable-final *n*, *frente*,

* Translator's note: The pronunciation of *z* and *c* (in *ce*, *ci*) like *s*.

razón, much more abundant than the initial, *noche, vino*, oc-cupies almost two-thirds of the proportion mentioned. The fre-quency of the *n* in Spanish and Portuguese is similar to that which this consonant has in Latin. It increases to nearly 8% in Italian, while in French, diminished by the vocalization of syllable-final nasals, it is reduced to 3%.

R single. Proportion, 5.91%. The most frequent position of this consonant is intervocalic, *oro*, which by itself alone repre-sents 2.40%. The rest is divided between the syllable-final and medial positions, *parte*, 1.64% and *prado*, 1.87%. The propor-tion corresponding to the double *rr* is not included here. In Spanish, as is well-known, it appears with its own value in phonetic and semantic differentiation.

L. More frequent as syllable-initial, *cielo*, than as final, *alto*. Total proportion, 5.46%. In French and Italian it occurs in similar proportion to Spanish. It was much less frequent in Latin, 2.50%. Its increase in Romance languages must result in large part from the frequent repetition of the forms of the article. In Portuguese, with the articles *o, a, os, as*, the *l* drops approximately to the same level it had in Latin.

D. It appears in Spanish almost as frequently as the *l*, 5.00%. The Spanish spoken by the common people diminishes the pro-portion of the *d* by eliminating this consonant in many cases where the literary pronunciation preserves it. The stop variant, *día, conde*, 1.22% is much less frequent than the fricative, *mudo*, 3.78%.

T. This consonant surrendered a large part of its field to *d*. From third place in the phonological series in Latin, with ap-proximately 9.00%, it came down in Spanish to the category of second rate sounds with a proportion of 4.82%. It presents an analogous reduction in Italian, French, and Portuguese, in which it shows proportions of 4.72%, 4.90%, and 5.06% re-spectively.

I. In the Spanish series, the vowel *i* appears in tenth place with a ratio of 4.75%. The transformation of the original phono-logical order has been so profound that this vowel, which stands at the front of the Latin system with a proportion of nearly 12%, does not figure in Spanish except as the last of the second category sounds. Among the Romance languages, Italian is the one that uses the *i* in much greater proportion, namely, 8.62%. Its percentage, however, does not equal that of the English *i*, whose proportion approaches nearly 10%—which puts this vowel in second place among Anglo-Saxon phonemes.[3]

A third category, with figures between three and one percent, is made up by the phonemes *k* (*c, q*), *m, p, b, z, u,* and voiced *g*. Altogether, the appearance of these seven elements in the phonetic composition of words is very much below that of the vowels *a* and *e* by themselves. Three voiceless consonants belong in this group, *k, p, z,* while in the first category only the *s* is of this type, and in the second, the *t*.

K. It includes *c, qu: casa, quinto.* Proportion 4.23%. The syllable-final *k, acto,* represents a small fraction, 0.13%, within this figure.

M. More frequent in syllable-initial position, *mesa, humo,* 2.40%, than in final position, *campo,* 0.69%. Total proportion 3.09%. In Latin it attained 8.66%, a higher proportion than it has in the Romance languages.

P. Less frequent than *t* and *k, paso, prisa.* Proportion, 3.06%. Extremely rare as syllable-final, *apto, concepto,* 0.02%.

B. It includes *b, v: boca, vida,* 2.54%. The bilabial fricative variant accounts for almost the entire frequency figure with 2.25%. The phonetic identification of the *v* with the *b* gives this phoneme a greater representation in Spanish than in other languages. In Italian the *b* represents 0.94% and the *v* 1.64%; in French, 1.82% and 3.46% respectively.

Z. Fricative interdental, *moza, decir,* 2.23%. Rare as final, *bizco, paz,* 0.06%. It is identified with the *s* in Andalusian and Spanish-American pronunciation, without losing its individuality as an orthoëpic archetype preserved in writing and in various manifestations of the literary tradition.

U. It is the vowel with the smallest representation in Spanish,

1.92%. In Latin, 4.62%. In Portuguese it has risen, at the expense of the *o*, to occupy second place, 7.62%, right after the *a* In French also the *u* (ou) is more frequent than in Spanish and Italian.

G. Voiced velar, *lengua, seguir*. Its rare appearance, 1.04%, corresponds almost entirely to the fricative variety. The participation of the stop in the aforementioned figure amounts to 0.08%.[4]

The phonemes whose frequency does not reach one percent make up the fourth and last category. At this small level figure the trilled *rr*, the labiodental *f*, the velar *j*, the palatals, *ll, y, ñ, ch*, and the extensive and varied list of the diphthongs and triphthongs of the language.

IE. It precedes in a favorable position the other Spanish diphthongs, *piedra, especie*, 0.86%. It is counted as a diphthong in *hielo, hierba*, although the *i* is generally pronounced in this position as a fricative or affricate *y*.

RR. Multiple trill, *rosa, honra, torre*. On account of the mechanics of its articulation it is considered as one of the most important difficulties for the foreign student. Its normal frequency, 0.80%, makes it appear, nevertheless, in one of the lowest degrees of the scale.

F. Its proportion in Spanish, 0.72%, is smaller than in French, Italian, and Portuguese, where it usually appears in a proportion greater than 3%. In English and German it is even more frequent than in the Romance languages.[5]

LL. As scarce in Spanish as in Portuguese and Italian, *llave, calle*, 0.60%. It is identified with the *y* in extensive Hispanic sections, *pollo: poyo*. It preserves its difference and sense in a general way in the orthoëpic representation of the language.

UE. Examples, *hueso, bueno*, 0.54%.

IA. Examples, *limpiar, desgracia*, 0.54%.

J. It amounts to very little in the entirety of the phonetic material, *hijo, elegir*, 0.51%. The analogous sound in German, *machen*, occurs in a proportion five times greater than in Spanish.

Y. Fricative or affricate palatal, *mayo, inyección,* 0.40%.

Ñ. Examples, *año, leña,* 0.36%. Also as scarce in French, Portuguese, and Italian.

IO. Examples, *sabio, perdió,* 0.32%.

CH. Last in the order of frequency among the Spanish consonants, *ocho, noche,* 0.30%.

In the lowest proportions, lower than 0.20%, come the diphthongs: AI, *aire;* EI, *veinte;* OI, *heroico;* AU, *causa;* EU, *feudo;* UA, *cuatro;* IU, *ciudad;* UI, *cuidado;* UO, *antiguo.* The most frequently used diphthongs are the rising type: *ie, ue, ia, io.*

Portuguese prefers the falling ones, *ai, au, ei, oi.* Among the several thousands of words examined there has not appeared any example at all of the diphthong *ou* or of the triphthongs *iai, iei, uai, uei.*[6]

The four established groups indicate the category of the phonemes with relation to their respective frequency. Along general lines, the order of these groups is the same in all the Romance languages. The principal vowels occupy first rank; the liquid and sibilant consonants, second; the stops, third; and the palatals the fourth.[7]

On this common basis, a peculiar characteristic of Spanish is the great frequency volume concentrated on the three vowels with the most open and voiced quality. The weak and the close vowels, which as has been noted, figure in other languages in relatively high proportion, appear in Spanish in very low proportion. It is worthy of note that the predominance of the *a* is found also in Basque in an even more marked way than in Spanish. The *a* occurs in Basque, according to my calculations, in a proportion of 15.70%.

Another outstanding feature of Spanish is the frequency of the *s.* In a passage of *Gloria,* Benito Pérez Galdós drew attention to the prominence with which in a conversation in a soft voice the muttering of the *s*'s stood out like foam on the waves. In another passage of Armando Palacio Valdés, this author mentions a boy who, in the monotony of collective prayer, amused himself by drawing out the *s*'s at the end of the sentences. The frication generally attenuated, and even aspirated in some regions, with which the syllable-final s is pronounced must be the cause of the fact that in current opinions concerning the phonetic qualities of Spanish, this is not considered a sibilant language.[8]

It can be noticed also in the preceding data the greater frequency of the voiced consonants b, d versus their respective voiceless ones, p, t, George K. Zipf pointed out the predominance of p, t, k over b, d, g in Sanskrit, Greek, Russian, German, and several other languages. Zipf and Francis M. Rogers found the same situation in their analyses of Latin, Italian, and French. Spanish, by showing a greater frequency of b, d, than of p, t, constitutes a peculiar case in which there are also certain points of agreement with Basque phonology.[9]

In the presentation of the phonemes b, d, g, the fricative variants predominate considerably over the stops. Catalan and Portuguese, although following an analogous road, present less difference than Spanish between these variants. The gentle and smooth quality of the fricative modalities of these profuse phonemes is an important element in the total effect of Spanish pronunciation:

	b	d	g
Stops	0.29%	1.22%	0.08%
Fricatives	2.25	4.02	0.96
Total	2.54%	5.24%	1.04%

The rr and the j are the two consonants whose pronunciation is generally given as a prime difficulty in Spanish classes for foreign students. The proportion of 0.80% and 0.51% with which these phonemes respectively appear indicates how small their role is in the whole of the language.

Palatal consonants, though numerous, exhibit rare frequency in the Romance languages. Spanish in particular makes very little use of this group of sounds. Centuries ago palatal sounds, which in the old language were represented by *x*, *g*, or *j* turned into the velar fricative represented today by the latter two phonemes.[10] While the palatal phonemes in Portuguese amount to 7.08%, in French 4.78%, and in Italian 3.74%, in Spanish they only represent 1.64%.

In the peculiar diminution of the *f* and the absence of *y*, Spanish varies from the phonological scheme of its linguistic group and appears once more in agreement with Basque.

The most frequent group of consonants is that of the alveolars *s*, *r*, *l*, *n*, with a proportion that reaches 26.45%. The only alveolar not included in the first categories is the multiple *rr*. Less numerous and frequent are the labials *p*, *b*, *m*, which represent 8.69%; the dentals *t*, *d*, 9.82%; and the velars *k*, *g*, *j*, 5.78%.

The total of the vowels reaches 40.33%; that of the diphthongs, 3.16%; that of the voiced consonants 33.14%; and that of the voiceless consonants, 23.37%. The individual figures corresponding to the phonemes of each group are summarized in the following table:

Vowels		Diphthongs	
a	13.00%	ie	0.86%
e	11.75	ia	0.54
o	8.90	ue	0.52
i	4.76	io	0.32
u	1.92	ua	0.20
	40.33%	ai	0.15
		ei	0.15
		oi	0.15
		au	0.09
		eu	0.05
		iu	0.05
		ui	0.05
		uo	0.03
		ou	0.00
			3.16%

Voiced consonants		Voiceless consonants	
n	6.94%	s	7.50%
r	5.91	t	4.82
l	5.46	k	4.23
d	5.00	p	3.06
m	3.09	z	2.23
b	2.54	f	0.72
g	1.04	j	0.51
s	1.00	ch	0.30
rr	0.80		23.37%
ll	0.60		
y	0.40		
ñ	0.36		
	33.14%		

The *s* figures as a normal phoneme among the voiceless consonants. It is included also, for reasons of phonetic calculation, in the series of the voiced consonants. Of course, the voiced *s*—the result of the influence of another voiced consonant immediately following, *rasgo, desnudo*—corresponds, from the phonological point of view, to the same general type of the *s*, the rating of which amounts to 8.50%.[11]

III.

Observations on the Spanish Vowels

THE FOLLOWING OBSERVATIONS are applicable not only to the Spanish vowels considered in the pronunciation peculiar to Castile. The circumstances pointed out here correspond for the most part to the general characteristics that these sounds display in all the countries in which Spanish is spoken. In the phonetic structure of the Spanish language, the vowels are a more stable and uniform element than the consonants. The differences of pronunciation between the Spanish of various countries affect the consonants more than the vowels. Nevertheless, a scrupulous analysis of the vowels, based especially on Castilian speech, cannot attribute universal value to all the details appreciable in the pronunciation of these sounds within the Hispanic world.[1]

The traditional teaching of Spanish orthoëpy used to present the five fundamental vowels as uniform and invariable sounds. Modern phonetics has pointed out the existence of distinct variants in the regular pronunciation of each one of these vowels. In essence, there is no contradiction between both teachings. From the point of view of their semantic function, the Spanish vowels in effect amount to the five phonemes cited. In the linguistic consciousness of the people who speak this language each vowel appears with only one single phonological representation.

Actually, modern phonetics has not discovered that Spanish possesses any greater number of vowels than those which have traditionally been taught. Its work has consisted simply in getting a more precise knowledge of the said phonemes. It has demonstrated that, far from displaying the uniformity of timbre which has been attributed to them, each one, under certain circumstances, undergoes perceptible changes that, without altering the phonological unity of the vowel or the semantic value of the words, influence the phonetic character of the language and the differentiation of the modalities of regional or dialectal speech.

These differences in the Spanish vowels are expressed with the same names used in other languages to distinguish their various vowel types. The designations of open and close vowels, however, are not used in Spanish with the full significance they ordinarily have in general phonetics. On the one hand, as has already been said, the open and close variants of a same vowel do not represent in Spanish individualized and distinct types within the phonological system of the language. On the other, the organic and acoustic measurements of these Spanish variants do not coincide exactly with the proportions given usually by phoneticians to distinguish open and close vowels in the table of cardinal values of these phonemes.

The timbre of the close types of the vowels *e* and *o* seems to display similar characteristics in all the area of the Romanic languages. A scrupulous analysis may find appreciable discrepancies in the phonetic operation of such sounds not only among the languages themselves but within the individual field of each one of them. But common experience bears witness on this point to essential coincidences that give a basis to the characterization of the generic types of the close vowels *e* and *o* as regular and sharply defined sounds in the general phonology of those languages. The investigations on linguistic geography dealing with the Romanic countries do not seem to have come up against any important obstacle to represent with uniform concepts and signs the phonetic forms corresponding to the aforementioned vowels.

In Spanish, the variants of *e* and *o* that are considered as close differ perceptibly from the general types assigned to such sounds. Rather than strictly close vowels, the Spanish variants are only medial sounds with a timbre more open and clear than that given by the *e* and the *o* to Spanish ears when pronounced by people of French or Italian tongue in words like *peso, canté, boda, pasó,* etc. Within the same peninsular territory, when the Catalans and the Portuguese speak Spanish, they, too, generally give the vowels *e, o* in words like the ones cited more close sounds than these vowels are heard with in Castile. In Catalan and Portuguese phonetics, it is usual to indicate the ordinary timbre of the close vowels *e, o* as equivalent to the one they have in Italian and French. The Spanish sounds corresponding to these vowels do not show that coincidence. The all-embracing inclusion of these sounds under the same formulas and signs with which the close vowels *e, o* are represented in those other languages would give an inaccurate idea of the phonetic reality of Spanish speech.

The different position of Spanish in relation to this matter becomes evident also by noting the quality of the open variants of those same vowels. The distance between these open variants and the close ones is less in Spanish than in the rest of the Romance languages. The difference of timbre Spanish displays between the *e* of *terco* and that of *peso*, or between the *o* of *borla* and that of *boda* does not constitute so clearly perceptible a contrast as it is in general the case in Italian, for example, between *festa* and *sapeva*, or in French between *porte* and *dos*. The variants *e* and *o* usually represented as open in phonetic transcriptions of Spanish pronunciation are actually semi-open sounds with an articulation intermediate between the forms previously mentioned—medial rather than close, as has been seen—and the strictly open types of Italian or French. The distance between such medial and semi-open variants is, nevertheless, perceptible and important enough in Spanish to be taken into account. Not only in the realm of linguistic studies but in the practical teaching of the pronunciation of this language as well.

On the other hand, Spanish does not use relaxed and colorless vowels analogous to the mute *e* of French or the unaccented *e* of Portuguese and Catalan. Unstressed vowels have generally in Catalan and Portuguese a sound less precise and defined than in Spanish. In Spanish vowels, the weak position with respect to the stress accent causes no doubt a certain degree of attenuation as to the clarity of sound. This modification, however, does never reach the point of causing these vowels to lose the essential character of the type they belong to. Even in Italian pronunciation the unstressed vowels seem to alter their acoustic quality more than in Spanish. It probably contributes to this the fact that Italian, like French, reduces the length of these vowels considerably while at the same time it lengthens the accented ones. The resulting difference between the two types of vowels is accordingly also greater than in current Spanish.

Portuguese possesses a complex vocalism in which mixed sounds with a vague and imprecise timbre play an important part. The influence of vowel metaphony reaches in Portuguese a more developed and active degree than in other languages. This causes the timbre of the accented vowel to get close and obscure when the final vowel of the same word is also a close sound. The influence that nasal consonants in Portuguese wield on the vowels is not limited to the simple nasalization of the original sounds. It also affects more profoundly their articulatory and acoustic quality. Unaccented vowels in Portuguese are frequently not only attenuated in the indicated manner, but also shortened and made voiceless, and in certain circumstances completely eliminated. The Portuguese vowel system, unlike the Spanish, is not distinguished by the regularity and precision of its sounds, but by the delicate mechanism of its changes and nuances. Galician vowels display clearer and more sharply defined characteristics than the Portuguese. Brazilian Portuguese, likewise, shows apparently on this point forms less complex and obscure than those of peninsular Portuguese.

In the vocalic system of Catalan the accented position makes open and clear sounds stand out, while outside of this position vowels take on, specially in the Catalan of Barcelona, obscure and relaxed forms. In some forms of Catalan the vowels *e* and *o* in the accented position reach ultra-open proportions. To the ear accustomed to the pronunciation of Castile, Catalan is distinguished by the relatively frequent use of vowels more open than the ordinary ones; while Portuguese stands out more specially by the predominance of close variants. The tendency to the opening of vowels is especially strong in Valencia, in some parts of the Balearic Islands, and in other areas of the Catalan linguistic territory. In many cases, vowels originally close as, for example, the stressed *e* of *cera* or *verde* and the *o* of *todo* and *flor*, are heard as close vowels in Portuguese, as fully open sounds in Valencian and Balearic dialect, and as intermediate forms, with medial or semi-open timbre, in Castilian territory. The position of each language in the relative degree of the vocalic timbre, as reflected in these examples, explains the fact that the contrast between the open and close variants of the vowels in question is less in Spanish than in Catalan and Portuguese.

Another phonetic characteristic that affects the vowels and shows different tendencies in these languages is that which concerns velarization. In a general way, the pronunciation of all Catalan and Portuguese sounds seems always more or less shaded with velar resonance. The basic point of articulation which could be considered as the center or axis of the phonological system of these languages seems to correspond to a more interior line of the articulatory field than that which serves as the usual base to Spanish pronunciation. The sound that can best be pointed out as an exponent of this difference is that of the velar *l*. In Portuguese and Catalan the syllable-final *l* represents a sound lower, more obscure, and farther back than that which the Spanish *l* presents in that same position. The velarization of the *a* in front of this *l* and in the other cases where such a variant of the *a* occurs, reaches too in Catalan and Portuguese a higher level than in Spanish. The effects of this tendency are manifested also in the mixed shade that the *a* and the front vowel *e, i* ordinarily acquire in Portuguese and Catalan in the unstressed position.

Within the realm of these languages, the resounding and velar articulation appears with more patent and more greatly developed characteristics in some regions than in others. Portuguese velarization gives the impression of being more intense and farther back than the Catalan. It is true that the fact that Portuguese sounds are produced in general with the jaws relatively closed can contribute to this impression. The opening angle of the jaws in Portuguese pronunciation is closer than in the Spanish, just as in Spanish it is closer than in Catalan. For this reason Catalan has a certain deep, resonant, and emphatic tone which is not usual in Portuguese. Deep and resonant speech shows greatly developed forms among some Valencian people. The velarization present in Galician, of the interior type of the Portuguese but more open and smoother, gives a touch of deep-toned effect to the pronunciation. The common basis of these effects is the tendency to give the posterior cavities of the vocal duct a greater amplitude than is ordinarily used in the articulation of Spanish sounds.

Velarization occurs in Spanish in special circumstances of affected expression. In the general typology of the voice, a throaty pronunciation has a lordly and aristocratic effect. The cut-off and hollow tone of the common pronunciation of Madrid is evidently the result of an attitude of affectation. In some places in the region of Murcia a peculiar pronunciation of the *ch* can be heard which tinges with a deep and emphatic timbre the immediately surrounding vowels. Outside of cases of this kind, there seems to be no Spanish regions where velarization takes place in the general way in which, with different aspects of articulation and development, it occurs in Galician-Portuguese and in Valencian-Catalan.

Following these observations, it is interesting to extend the comparison to the Basque vowels. Outside of the Suletine Basque dialect, in French Biscay, which possesses the sound of the *ü*—labialized palatal—received probably from French, the other Basque dialects, in France and Spain, employ vowels identical with those of Spanish. The Basque *e* and *o* coincide with the Spanish ones in the essential characteristics of their articulation and timbre. Basque, like Spanish, does not possess open and close variants of these vowels with distinct phonological import. The sound with which the said vowels are pronounced in Basque is not that of the close or open types the *e* and *o* have in French, Italian, Catalan, or Portuguese, but that of the Spanish *e* and *o*—medial in some cases and semi-open in others. The phonetic features that concur in the differentiation of these medial and semi-open variants coincide also fundamentally in Spanish and in Basque.

Basque does not have mixed and relaxed vowels as do Portuguese and Catalan, nor nasalized vowels as French and Portuguese. Basque thus is as strange as Spanish to the interior mode of articulation and to the velar resonance of Portuguese and Catalan. The similarity of the Basque vowels to the Spanish ones has been noted by people of diverse origins. Basque and Spanish vowels sound, in effect, alike, although etymologically and morphologically the words in which such sounds are heard have no relation one with the other. Without any need of special preparation in this matter, the Spanish ear recognizes that Spanish spoken by the Basques fits the pronunciation of Castile more closely than that heard from the lips of Catalans, Valencians, or Galicians. Applying spontaneously the same phonetic habits of their regional speech, the Basque accurately gives the pronunciation of the Spanish vowels the degree of openness, tension, and quality that corresponds to them. Only at the cost of long practice and careful attention do the Catalans, Valencians, and natives of the Balearic Islands, avoid, when speaking Spanish, their tonic *e* and *o*, at times too open and at times too close; and their stressed *a*, in some cases palatal, tense, and wide-open, and in others velar, low, and obscure, as well as their unstressed *a* and *e*, of an indistinct and vacillating timbre. It is equally difficult for the Galicians to adapt themselves to Spanish pronunciation, in which the word-final vowels *e* and *o* have a more open timbre than in their own language, and to clear up in general the character of their articulation, which has fewer movements and is shaded with inner resonances. The Basques, on the other hand, native speakers of a language fundamentally distinct from the rest of the peninsular languages, are nevertheless the ones who most easily and thoroughly apprehend the heart of a matter of such subtle nature and of such essential function in the characterization of Spanish phonology.

It is not probable that this correspondence has been produced by Castilianization of the Basque vowel system nor by the influence of the Basque on the Castilian system either. It should be sufficient to note that the similarities indicated refer not only to the Spanish-Basque dialects but to the French-Basque ones also. Throughout the whole Basque domain the vowels display an essentially uniform character. Neither Labortano, nor Low Navarrese, nor Suletino itself—besides the aforementioned case of the *ü*—have adapted their vowels to the types and forms of the French vowel system. Phonetic differences among the Basque dialects affect specially, as in Spanish, the pronunciation of the consonants. Quite well-known, besides, is the constancy of Basque in the preservation of its linguistic peculiarities as well as the existence in its phonological repertory of consonant sounds whose articulation has no equivalent in French or in Spanish phonetics.

On the other hand, since both peoples are so closely related by historic and geographic ties, the idea that the similarities between the Spanish and the Basque vowels are purely coincidental, without any connection of kinship or of common tradition, cannot seem convincing. The precision and clarity observed in the timbre of these sounds may be signs of a definite and ancient tradition. The Spanish vowel system seems to have established itself centuries ago in essentially uniform patterns. There are tendencies toward assimilation, dissimilation, and reduction of hiatus that affect unstressed vowels specially and that have been operative at all times and continue operating on the phonetic makeup of some words; but the existence of these phenomena does not imply vagueness or vacillation in regard to the quality of the sounds themselves. In the century of the Cid's minstrel, as in that of Alfonso the Wise, of Juan Ruiz, the Archpriest of Hita, of Elio Antonio de Nebrija, or of Miguel de Cervantes, Spanish vowels were heard probably with the same sounds with which they are pronounced today. What can be deduced from the writing of the rhymes, from the references of the writers, or from popular tradition, indicates that throughout the centuries the language must have undergone no appreciable modification on this point.

The peculiar nature of Basque and Spanish vowels is found also perhaps in dialectal pockets of France bordering on Basque. Unfortunately, neither the Linguistic Atlas of France nor the studies devoted to the dialectal speech of those places offer sufficiently detailed information on this matter. It is well-known that the interest of linguistic investigation has put in general more attention on the historical evolution of sound than on the minute description of their phonetic characteristics. Spanish-Basque vowels, with their special physiognomy of medial and semiopen sounds, are distinguished without any great effort from the normal types of open and close vowels. Let us hope that some day the area of these Spanish-Basque vowels will be properly defined in its French as well as in its peninsular boundaries. One point on which Gascon appears of course in disagreement with the tradition these facts represent is the persistence in this dialect of the phonological duality of open and close types of the vowels *e* and *o*. Nevertheless, there may be sections of that same region where the deep Iberian substratum these facts suggest may be reflected in the vowels as well as in other characteristics of Gascon pronunciation. In Spain, the extension of the Castilian vowels includes Aragon and reaches up to part of Catalonia and Valencia; but it does not entirely include Extremadura or Andalusia. In the Spanish-American countries, judging by information being constantly gained on the matter, the pronunciation of vowels shows likewise certain differences between some regions and others without affecting the fundamental unity of their phonetic types.

It is understandable that the pronunciation of vowels has always been a subject specially sensitive to the tendencies of the linguistic substratum of the people. Modern experience has told us much about the influence that the phonetic habits of the mother language exercise on the perception and imitation of the sounds of another language. Generally, such sounds are interpreted by making them correspond to the ones they resemble most among those the individual is familiar with in his own language. On trying to reproduce the foreign sound, the phonetic form given to it tends to accommodate itself to the local phoneme considered its equivalent. The basis for this approximate adaptation is the relatively flexible nature of the phoneme itself, whose linguistic unity, as is known, permits its pronunciation to offer different variants. In bilingual regions, the pronunciation of the official or national language adapts itself ordinarily to the individual phonetics of the speech of every such region. When the local speech fades gradually from the use of the people, its phonetic traits remain nevertheless impressed on the language that took its place. In the reflection of its vowel sound, the ancient and extinct Iberian tongue must have transmitted to the new Romanic speech a part of its euphonic tradition. The local stamp of Cantabrian Latin, the neighbor of resistant Basque-Iberian, remained no doubt in the tendencies that have modeled the quality of the vowels and other elements of the speech of Castile.

Dialectal evolution in regions of Spain and Spanish America still not well defined shows signs that indicate the beginning of an important modification in the five single-vowel phonemes system of Spanish. This phenomenon arises from the phonetic transformation caused in those regions by the loss of the hereditary aspiration of the word-final *s* and *z*.

The aspiration of these consonants is in general weaker and more tenuous in word-final than in medial position. Frequently, such a final aspiration comes out not with its original voiceless timbre, but as a light voiced breath which at times seems to be a mere prolongation of the preceding vowel, with the disappearance of all perceptible remains of the aspirated element.

My observations on this matter, expounded in the homage to Trubetzkoy, of the *Cercle linguistique de Prague* and in the *Revista de Filología Hispánica*, Buenos Aires, 1939, were limited to Andalusian pronunciation. Before the voiceless aspiration of final *s* and *z* of general Andalusian, the vowel of the same final syllable acquires a relatively open timbre. This increases its degree of opening when the aspiration becomes voiced, a frequent happening in popular Andalusian speech. When this aspiration disappears, the vowel keeps its open timbre thus assuming the semantic function corresponding to the eliminated *s* and *z*.

As a result of such a change, words apparently reduced to a same form maintain their semantic differentiation by means of the timbre of their respective final vowel. The phonemic value of this vowel allows the distinction, for example, between *dio*, a verb, with middle timbre *o* and *dio(s)*, a noun, with open *o*, as well as between *perdí*, the verb, with middle *i*, and *perdi(z)*, the noun, with open *i*.

The differentiation is particularly active between singular and plural: *boca, casa, puerta*, with middle *a*, and *boca(s), casa(s), puerta(s)* with *a* more open and farther back; *pie, diente, peine*, with middle *e*, and *pie(s), diente(s), peine(s)*, with open *e*; *pelo, toro, campo*, with middle *o*, and *pelo(s), toro(s), campo(s)*, with open *o*.

The phonemic distinction takes place likewise in the conjugation of verbs between the second and the third person of some tenses of the verb: *va, canta, iba, tendrá, diga, viera*, with final middle *a*, and *va(s), canta(s), iba(s), tendrá(s), diga(s), viera(s)*, with a more open and farther back *a*; *viene, pierde, cante, llegue*, with final middle *e*, and *viene(s), pierde(s), cante(s), llegue(s)*, with open *e*.

These observations have been confirmed, after the publication of my first data, in studies undertaken by other investigators on the speech of certain localities of Andalusia.[2] It is only natural that this same phenomenon should also be observed in like manner in the rest of the dialect regions in which aspiration and elimination of the final *s* and *z* has taken place. The loss of these consonants has been attested in regions of Mexico, New Mexico, Guatemala, Nicaragua, El Salvador, Colombia, Ecuador, Peru, etc. However, the information has failed to be specific concerning the timbre of the vowels possibly affected by such a loss. A more thorough observation will probably discover a phonemic doubling analogous to that which has developed in Andalusian. For my part, I proved the existence of this fact in the popular speech of Puerto Rico.[3]

It is to be noticed that the influence of the lost aspiration does not restrict itself to how open it makes the affected vowel. There are signs of this vowel becoming not only more open but also somewhat longer than the corresponding average type. There is too a certain intensity or vibratory buzzing that is no doubt a vestige, as the lengthening itself, of the lost voiced aspiration. Besides the greater opening of the timbre, the slight reinforcement of quantity and sonority gives the vowel of the plural a relatively clearer and tenser sound than in the singular—*diente*, *diente(s)*—and so to that of the second person with respect to the third—*va, va(s)*.

In truth, this new situation has not yet reached the stage of being precisely defined in the dialectal consciousness. The preservation of final *s* and *z*, their voiced or voiceless aspiration, and the total loss of the aspiration all occur together in the same localities. Each case corresponds to a definite social level, but there exists among all of them intimate communication and contact. Within this relationship, the contrast between the mentioned vocalic modalities, with their acoustic and semantic distinctions, acts in a more or less unconscious manner. It does not quite reach the level of a properly phonological phenomenon.

One can think of the possibility that, in due time, the differentiating role such variants play may lead to their complete phonemic individualization. However, it may perhaps be more probable that the stream of the official literary language prevents their development and reduces them to the phonetic identity that is observed, for example, in the French *fille, filles; jour, jours*. Worthy of note in this connection, is the illustration afforded within the same Andalusian field by vowels affected by the loss of final *l* or *r* in examples like *so* (sol), *flo* (flor), *papé* (papel), *cantá* (cantar). One notices that these vowels, in spite of belonging to the open type, do not show this quality to the extent of those influenced by the elimination of aspirated *s* and *z*; neither do they manifest the lengthening nor the vibrating nuance also evident in the latter.

One can perceive, in effect, that the *e* of *mie* (miel) and that of *mie* (mies) are not identical, although both are open; likewise, that of *pie* (piel) differs from that of *pie* (pies), without getting confused with that of the singular *pie*. It seems that upon being out of the frame of the checked syllable by the disappearance of *l* and *r*, the vowels of *sol*, *flor*, *papel*, etc., not pressed by the articulatory and morphological influence of the final *s*, have turned away in a relatively moderate degree from their respective average types. In the cases resulting from the loss of this *s*, the dialectal inclination can be likewise obliged to reduce and blur a phonemic differentiation essentially opposed to the traditional tendency of Spanish vocalism toward simplicity and uniformity.

IV.

Syllabic Types

THE FREE SYLLABLE can consist of a simple vowel or of a vowel or diphthong to which one or two preceding consonants are joined: *a–bri–go, la–bio, cri–a–do*. The checked syllable is one that adds one or two consonants after the vowel: *pas–tor, ins–crip–ción, cons–truc–tor*. The most general type in Spanish consists of the free syllable formed by a consonant and a vowel: *bo–ca, pa–so, ma–ña–na*. The alternating sequence of consonant and vowel harmonizes the phonological balance of the syllabic nuclei. This feature is altered by the divisive vacuum of vowels in hiatus and by the cumulative clustering of consonants.[1]

Spanish has always tried to reduce the occurrence of hiatus and of consonant clusters. Aside from old procedures like those performed in *reina, ley, ser*, present-day pronunciation ordinarily simplifies some juxtapositions of vowels which in other languages maintain their etymological hiatus: *coexistir, teología, violín*. Forms with several consonants together, like *transmite, subscriptor*, occur in Spanish with orthoëpic plenitude only in affected language. Current speech reduces the number of such groups by means of the abbreviation or elimination of one or another of its elements.

The proportion in which each type of syllable figures in the modern language appears in the following percentages, obtained from texts representative of ordinary style:

1.	ba: *ca—mi—no*	58.45%
2.	bab: *mar—tes*	27.35
3.	a: *y, o, a*	5.07
4.	bba: *tri—ple*	4.70
5.	ab: *él, es*	3.31
6.	bbab: *plan, tres*	1.12
7.	abb: *obs*—tá—cu—lo	0.00
8.	babb: *pers*—pi—caz	0.00
9.	bbabb: *trans*—cri—bir	0.00
		100.00

The last three forms are so little used that they have not provided one single example in the texts on which these data are based.

The fact that the syllables are more or less replete with vowels or consonants influences the phonological effect of the word. Fernando de Herrera, aware of the advantage which poetry can obtain in certain cases from the ligatures of hiatus, practiced his theory in examples such as "Sus odi—osos pasos imitaste," "Entre el rigor de Marte vi—olento."

The checked syllable, by its own nature, gives density to the effect of the articulation; its implosive movement supports the final impression of the closest phoneme; the vowel nucleus of the syllable appears influenced by the effect of the adjacent consonant, which in turn remains as suspended at the end of the dynamic unit it belongs to. Concurrently, the free syllable represents a rising effort which attains its greatest perceptibility in the vowel with which its respective unit ends. The increasing angle of the free syllable gives a forward direction to its opening, while in the checked syllable the depression of the final consonant restrains the voiced impulse which has as its center the preceding vowel. The dominant habit of the free syllable produces in Spanish the syntactic linking of the final consonant with the vowel that follows it, while in English even the word-medial intervocalic consonant is ordinarily attracted to the first of the clusters among which it is located. In Spanish, the dominant quality of the syllables gives the articulatory activity the character of a successive series of opening movements; in English it is that of a succession of implosions of repressed sonority.

Spanish does not have syllables in which the vowel is followed by more than two consonants, as in English *first, facts, worlds, attempts.* Syllables with two consonants after the vowel appear in Spanish only in medial position. There are not in Spanish today words that end in more than one consonant, like the old *puent, muert.* The consonants that at the present time play the most apparent part at the end of words are *s, l, n, r, z, d.* Spanish words ending in a consonant represent an average of 38%; while in English this type of vocable appears on any page in a proportion not less than 67%.

The *s* is the most frequent word-final consonant. The plural ending contributes specially to this. The repetition of the articles *el, un* causes the *l* and the *n* to attain important figures too as final phonemes. The final *r* is found in lower proportion, although it has the assistance of the infinitives. In the last places of this series we have *z* and *d.* Only in rare cases is any other final consonant found, as in *boj, cenit.* The *m* of *álbum, máximum* is currently pronounced as *n.*[2]

The effects of alliteration of consonants are, therefore, very rare in Spanish. English phraseology and metrics, on the other hand, employ them very much.[3] Nevertheless, examples in poetry and prose are found with some frequency in which checked syllables, in accordance with the emphasis of the respective passages, heighten the support of the accent by lengthening the consonants. The phonemes that on account of the natural resonance of their particular articulation lend themselves better to this end are the nasal *m* and *n*; as in the following lines of Fernando de Herrera:

> Por la gloria debida de tu nombre,
> por la venganza de tu muerta gente.

In a passage of similar dramatic stress, Federico García Lorca also gave insistent support to the medial vibration of these same phonemes:

> El llanto es un perro inmenso.
> El llanto es un violín inmenso.
> Las lágrimas amordazan al viento
> y no se oye otra cosa que llanto.

The effect of the roll of the *rr*, employed in several passages, is associated expressively with the nasal in the familiar example of Nicasio Gallego:

> Rueda allá rechinando la cureña,
> aca retumba el espantoso trueno.[4]

Cervantes, to the effect of the nasals, added the feeling of polysyllabic and oxytonical vocables in most of the names, at once high-sounding and humorous, with which he designated the princes imagined by don Quixote with the flocks he took for armies. The prosodic magnificence of these names contrasts with the ironical intention of their semantic allusions: Brandabarbarán de Boliche, Alfeñiquén del Algarbe, Pentapolín del Arremangado Brazo, Alifanfarrón de la Trapobana.

There is no question that the sibilant articulation of the *s*, so insistently repeated, helps to evoke the murmuring quiet of the grove in which Garcilaso placed the scene of his third eclogue:

> En el silencio sólo se escuchaba
> un susurro de abejas que sonaba.

It is the vowels more than the consonants that lend themselves in Spanish to the contrasts or harmonies of timbre that in certain cases strengthen or soften the expression. The same applies to the correlation between the sonorous quality of the words and the temper or color of the emotion that inspires them.[5] The solemn tone with which the *u* appears so many times in the poetry of San Juan de la Cruz cannot be considered alien to the sentiments of the poet. Nor can it be by mere chance either that the pathetic tone of Fernando de Herrera's elegy to the loss of King Sebastian rests so many times, at key points of the verses, on the sombre note of the *o*—repeated specially in the first stanza of the composition, in expressions like "voz de dolor," "desnuda de valor," "asombre con horror." The sound of the *i*, repeated in and out of the rhyme in Lope the Vega's sonnet on Lucinda and the fugitive little bird in many words like *portillo, libre, suspiro, mejillas, amarillo, nido, peligro, ligas, pico, enternecido*, impresses its diminutive and palatal timbre on the entire composition. A passage in which Lope's mastery for putting these effects into play is revealed is the following gloss of *tí* and *tú*, a model of anticipated vanguardism:

> Es el *tí* diminutivo
> del *tú*, y es hijo del *mí*,
> porque le regala ansí
> con el acento más vivo.
> El *tú* es bajo, y tiple el *mí*
> *Tú* manda, *tú* desafía,
> *tú* es trompeta, *tú* es cochero.
> *Tí* es clarín, *tí* es chirimía,
> y por eso al *tú* no quiero
> sino a *tí* que lo eres mía.

Lope puts this gloss in the mouth of the acolyte Pedro, an old student of Latin, in *La esclava de su galán*, act III, scene 7, as a commentary to the declaration with which the gallant don Juan tries to dispel the jealousy of doña Elena: "I shall never see her in my life—but you who are my very own." After this scene, the glossed phrase comes back repeatedly to the mind of the lady on reviewing the impressions of their meeting.

V.

Lexical Types

THE PHONOLOGICAL INDIVIDUALITY of a word includes its stress form and its semantic function. The number of syllables and the place of the stress give each vocable a definite structure with which it influences the phonetic totality of the sentence. Simultaneously, the logical category to which words belong affects the level and density of the mental line of the utterance. The habits of everyday language cause the words to present diverse proportions in each one of these two aspects.

In the texts examined for this purpose, the stress types to which the words belong by reason of the combination of stress and number of syllables appeared in the following order:

1. Bisyllabic paroxytones: *casa*   17.53%
2. Trisyllabic paroxytones: *camino*   14.93
3. Accented monosyllables: *luz*   7.54
4. Bisyllabic oxytones: *razón*   5.69
5. Tetrasyllabic paroxytones: *verdadero*   5.45
6. Trisyllabic oxytones: *corazón*   3.79
7. Trisyllabic proparoxytones: *rápido*   0.95
8. Tetrasyllabic oxytones: *reconocer*   0.71
9. Tetrasyllabic proparoxytones: *capítulo*   0.71
10. Pentasyllabic paroxytones: *comprometido*   0.71
11. Pentasyllabic oxytones: *administración*   0.47
12. Pentasyllabic proparoxytones: *antimonárquico*   0.24

13. Hexasyllabic paroxytones: *contraproducente*   0.24
14. Unstressed monosyllables: *la, en*   38.43
15. Unstressed bisyllables: *desde*   2.61
                                                    ————
                                                    100.00

The paroxytones add up to 38.86%; the oxytones, without counting the stressed monosyllables, to 10.66%; the proparoxytones, 1.90%; the unstressed words, 41.04%. Sixty percent of the usual lexicon is formed by stressed words of one, two, or three syllables. Bisyllabic and trisyllabic paroxytones predominate specially. Words of more than four syllables show a very low proportion. In the texts examined words of more than six syllables did not appear.

All things being equal with respect to the totality of the utterance, oxytones, with the expiratory prominence of their final syllable, seem more forceful than the paroxytones. The rhyming of oxytones is called masculine rhyme, and that of paroxytones, feminine rhyme. The unstressed ending of paroxytones diminishes the effect of the strong syllable and facilitates and smoothes phonetic linking. The definite asseveration emphasizes its firmness when the sentence ends with an oxytone. It is probable that the proportion of this type of word increases in passages of an authoritarian or dramatic tone and decreases in those of ingratiating and persuasive intent. The proparoxytones contain in themselves a certain emphasis which in part is the result of the learned character of the majority of these words, even when the basis of such an effect resides principally in dactyllic accentuation, the preferred rhythm of national anthems. Unstressed words, despite their high frequency index, play a secondary role. For the most part, they are, as everybody knows, articles, prepositions, and conjunctions. The expressive tension diminishes when these function words are repeated and multiplied excessively in the stream of speech.

The phonological image of words is specially influenced by the effect resulting from the combination of their vowels. The most important function on this point corresponds to the stressed vowels and to the unstressed finals. The action of vocalic harmony, however, may reach out also to other positions. Certain types of assonances and similicadences are present in the language with abundant lexical material, while other combinations are noted by their scarcity. As seen in the stream of ordinary speech, the frequency of these types does not resemble the case of chapters of rhyme dictionaries where, on the one hand, identities are restricted by the coincidence of the consonants, and on the other, all kinds of words are admitted. In the prose texts these observations refer to, the classification of stressed words, among the twenty vowel combinations of the final syllables, has produced the following results:

á–o:	paso, estado	9.12%
é–o:	cielo, vemos	8.56
á–a:	clara, llegaba	8.35
í–a:	vida, tenía	8.24
é–a:	estrella, deja	7.86
ó:	razón, perdió	7.45
á:	verdad, saldrá	7.29
á–e:	padre, vale	6.68
í–o:	camino, hizo	5.52
é:	papel, tener	5.08
é–e:	gente, debe	4.82
ó–a:	boca, toda	4.32
ó–e:	hombre, torpe	3.55
ú–a:	luna, escucha	3.43
ó–o:	ojo, poco	3.20
í:	allí, salir	2.15
ú–o:	nudo, oscuro	2.08
í–e:	triste, dice	1.55
ú:	virtud, azul	0.55
ú–e:	nube, sube	0.20

$$100.00$$

Although in the above-mentioned texts some differences are observed in the proportion of each case, the general lines of the scale in which the words are arranged according to the subject in point are repeated with surprising regularity. The paroxytone combinations with *a* and *e* in the stressed syllable and *o*, *a* in the final predominate. The combinations *á–o*, *é–o*, and *á–a* vie for first place. For second position *í–a*, *é–a*, *ó* and *á* compete also. In paroxytones which have *o* in their stressed syllable, *ó–a*, *ó–e*, *ó–o*, the frequency index drops greatly. The paroxytones in *í–e*, *ú–e*, and the oxytones in *ú* appear in last place in all the texts examined. It is understandable that the practices observed in the rhymes of poetry are not alien to the linguistic conditions these facts show, whether it is a question of the spontaneous manifestations of popular metrical composition, or a matter of the artistic tendencies and effects of learned versifications.

The proportion in which the grammatical elements combine within a text influences its phonological character to a considerable extent. From this point of view, the proportional representation with which each category of words generally appears in current Spanish is indicated in the following series:

Nouns	24.18%
Adjectives	11.00
Verbs	13.33
Adverbs	6.11
Pronouns	6.11
Articles	14.54
Prepositions	18.07
Conjunctions	6.66
	100.00

As has already been stated, these data are based on magazine and newspaper articles and narrative selections from modern novels not noted for stylistic peculiarities. One must realize that artistic prose and poetic language do not precisely follow the figures here pointed out. The percentage of verbs will be, without doubt, greater in texts in which dynamic action prevails over descriptive elements. The use of adjectives will show higher proportions in the cases where literary elaboration cultivates and reinforces qualitative description. Syntax of a shorter design must make less use of the linking particles than compositions of long and complex sentences.

Nouns are the most frequently used vocables in the construction of sentences. Their proportion equals one-fourth of all words. The sizes of all the texts have regularly remained between 22 and 27%. In second place come the prepositions, more abundant than conjunctions and articles. The definite article is more frequent than the indefinite. Verbs and adjectives are far below nouns. Adverbs and pronouns, including stressed and unstressed forms, are the least frequent categories. Among nouns, the masculine substantives prevail over the feminines, and the singular forms over the plurals. Although gender and number depend naturally on the subject treated, the examination of several texts of ordinary style indicates that each hundred nouns give the following groups:

	Masculines	
In −*o*:	cuerpo	36.06%
In −*e*:	hombre	6.15
In −*a*:	poeta	3.05
In consonant:	árbol	9.53
		54.79%
	Feminines	
In −*a*:	puerta	30.76
In −*e*:	fuente	3.07
In consonant:	luz	11.38
		45.21%

In the texts examined there were no examples of feminines in −*o, mano, nao,* or of nouns of any gender ending in *i* or *u*.

VI.

The Role of Quantity

As an element which does not exercise an active influence on the meaning of words, quantity might remain outside the phonological scheme of the Spanish language. It is well-known that in this language, in contrast to what happens in certain instances in English and German, giving the vowels or the syllables greater or lesser length is a matter unconnected with the semantic value assigned to each word. It is necessary, nevertheless, to recognize that quantity maintains its influence in the configuration and measurement of the most important units within the phonological constitution of the language.

The laws of quantity, which Friedrich Diez attributed in a general way to the vowels of the Romance languages, are indeed fulfilled in Spanish within certain restrictions. Naturally long vowels, with the relative duration implied by such a concept in the languages where these sounds exist, are not usually heard in current Spanish except in special cases. Johan Storm was right when he pointed out that a characteristic feature of Spanish pronunciation is the brevity of its vowels, whatever the degree of stress of these sounds may be and the form of the syllables in which they appear.

It is however, a matter of a brevity in which a variety of shades is produced. In the stressed vowels one is ordinarily aware of a certain greater length as compared with those in weak syllables. The maximum reduction occurs usually in the penultimate vowels of proparoxytones. With the aid of the high tones of anticadences and semianticadences, the unstressed finals attain sometimes greater length than those which bear the stress. In the series of weak vowels which frequently result from the syntactic succession of unstressed particles, differences of duration related to the alternating movement of the expiratory effort appear also. No vowel is shortened so much, besides the modifications caused by the hiatus reduction in some cases, as to become muffled or silenced. The following example will give an idea of the differences of vowel quantity in a sentence recorded and measured with the aid of the kymograph. The figures indicate in hundredths of seconds the duration of each vowel:

Co	ro	na	das	de	pám	pa	nos	y	flo	res
6	6	12	8	5	9	5	8	5	14	10

In dialectal pronunciation there are slower or faster modalities that alter the indicated conditions. There are Andalusians who lengthen now and then certain vowels of each sentence and pass lightly over the other sounds, syllables, or words enclosed between such emphases. There are other people of Andalusia, however, whose articulation is deliberate, with the duration of the vowels more evenly distributed. In some regions of the north of Spain, and specially in Aragon, the lengthening of final unstressed vowels is characteristic, even in instances in which the ending of the sentences and the falling of the tone give rise in other localities to the reduction and relaxation of these same sounds.

Obvious too are the differences between the various Spanish-American accents in reference to the tempo or beat of the utterance and the quantitative relation of the sounds. Such modifications of the spoken word, so important for the characterization of the speech of each country, can be measured easily. The particular impression that the words give according to the nature or origin of the people who pronounce them is to a large extent the product of the length proportions with which the sounds combine. Spanish Americans interested in these studies will surely try in time to discover, with the precision modern phonetics affords, these intimacies of their manner of speech.[1]

Concerned by the quantitative system of classic metrics, authors of treatises on orthoëpy and prosody have long talked about long and short syllables. Ignacio de Luzán and J. Gómez Hermosilla are the most outstanding names among the writers who tried to see in the Spanish syllables conditions analogous to those which served as the rhythmic basis of Greek and Latin poetry. The habit, not yet disappeared, of confusing quantity and accent in the same concept, calling strong syllables long and weak ones short, has been even more current. A third group is constituted by some who deny the possibility of imitating quantitative versification and end by saying that in Spanish syllables have practically the same length.

Radio announcers, required altogether too frequently to read a very great amount of commercials and news items in a given time, produce a kind of Spanish in which the syllables must each come out practically with the same length. This hurried and clipped pronunciation is in fact characteristic of radio announcers in all languages. Through this type of accelerated and profitably conceived broadcasts, all languages acquire the same inexpressive mechanical tone. Quite other is the case with dramatic actors, among whom the cultivation of correct and fine speech has always been an all-time tradition. It is to be regretted that in radio communication, of much greater range and diffusion, the necessary volume of commercial advertisements forces a lack of attention to the quality of the expression and to the care and respect that the language and the very effectiveness of such activities deserve.

Neither in common speech nor in literary pronunciation are Spanish syllables of an equal length. In the experimental measurement of some common words, syllables of ten or twelve hundredths of a second appear next to others of twenty or twenty-five. In declamation and speeches, short syllables of eight, ten, or twelve hundredths alternate with others which at times reach even fifty hundredths.[2] Many have denied that in

Spanish syllables there are differences in quantity in the proportion of 1:2. The evidence of objective and first-hand investigation shows that in certain cases such differences reach a proportion of 1:3 and 1:4.

These variations in syllabic quantity, while not affecting the ideologic value of the words, are specially important in the representation of other not less essential elements. The lengthening of the normal duration of a word emphasizes its meaning; shortening dissipates and attentuates it. The syllables of an entreaty are prolonged and softened; those of a command are shortened and strengthened; those of indecision are kept hesitant. Diction is slowed down in sententious and learned phrases. There is no attitude or change of mood which does not affect the vibrations of quantity, no less sensitive to these effects than those of stress or tone.

Besides the conditions of emotional expression, the whole structure of the sentence responds to the basic dimensions established by the habits of every language. Stress groups as well as melodic units are based on proportions that constitute the center of their respective circles. In poetry specially, quantity is always an essential factor, even when its manifestations are not governed by the norms of Greco-Latin tradition. Stress rhythm, with its combinations of tempos, anacruses, ceasures, and pauses, has as its basis the regularity of intervals. In certain rhythmic effects, stress can appear supported or substituted by other elements of a phonetic, morphological, or semantic order. Only quantitative proportion remains in the last analysis as a substantial condition of the nature of rhythm.

VII.

Stress and Lack of Stress

THE EXPIRATORY or stress accent is an essential part of the characterization and differentiation of Spanish words. The sense of the phonological importance of this aspect of the sounds seems to have had a special vital influence throughout all stages of the language. It can be noted that this same sense is perhaps the point on which there is today the greatest agreement in the speech of all Hispanic peoples. The differences and peculiarities of regional pronunciations rarely alter the place on which each word receives the stress support. The change of stress from one syllable to another, permitted with certain freedom in other languages, takes place in Spanish only within the design of its semantic function.

Most Spanish words have a unique and invariable stress. Any error in stress deforms the normal configuration of the words to the point of making them in some cases unrecognizable. In other cases, the word, having the same form as far as the phonemes which constitute it is concerned, changes its morphological and significative value according to the syllable in which the stress is placed. Such transformations abound in the inflection of verbs:

miro, present	*miró*, preterit
llame, subjunctive	*llamé*, preterite
rogara, pluperf.	*rogará*, fut. ind.
llegare, fut. subj.	*llegaré*, fut. ind.

On occasions the phonological contrast of stress occurs between nouns and verbs:

ira, noun	*irá*, future
veras, noun	*verás*, future
andén, noun	*anden*, subjunctive
grano, noun	*granó*, preterit

The stress contrast goes sometimes so far as to differentiate, among apparently identical words, three forms of different meaning, as the following well-known examples show:

límite	*limite*	*limité*
cántara	*cantara*	*cantará*
ánimo	*animo*	*animó*
depósito	*deposito*	*depositó*

Another abundant source of differentiation is the antithesis which results from the presence or absence of the stress in words constituted by the same sounds:[1]

tú, pronoun	*tu*, posses. adj.
sí, adverb	*si*, conjunction
dé, verb	*de*, preposition
té, noun	*te*, pronoun
mí, pronoun	*mi*, posses. adj.

Stress and lack of stress appear in close relation to the logical category to which the word belongs. On that of stress, we find in general the nouns, pronouns, verbs, and adverbs; on that of lack of stress, the articles, prepositions, and conjunctions. Certain words that ordinarily belong to the first category descend to the second when used in syntactical relations of a secondary character. The loss of the stress is an indication of the transition of the word from a substantive hierarchy to an instrumental role:

Stressed	Unstressed
sobre, noun or verb	*sobre*, preposition
bajo, adjective	*bajo*, preposition
luego, adverb	*luego*, conjunction
más, adverb	*mas*, conjunction
aún, adverb	*aun*, conjunction

It is not easy to explain why the language has extended the habit of maintaining or suppressing the stress accent to the possessives *nuestro* and *vuestro*, as they are pronouns or adjectives, while the demonstratives *este, ese, aquel* are ordinarily pronounced in both cases as stressed words. The reduction of the adjectives *mi, tu, su* indicates conditions in the origin and history of these forms different from those of the other pronouns. Usage is not too consistent on this point. While there are regions in the north of Spain where the possessive adjectives keep their stress, there are also certain other not too well defined areas of the Peninsula, and of Spanish America too, where demonstrative adjectives are pronounced more or less decidedly as unstressed forms.

In such nouns as *padre, madre, tío, hermano, santo,* etc. placed before proper nouns as a form of address; in those functioning as prepositive elements in locutions of adverbial character, like *cuesta arriba, boca abajo, cara al cielo*; and in the qualifiers that precede the central forms in vocative phrases, like ¡*Buen hombre*! ¡*Mala cabeza*!, both semantic descent and loss of stress take place at the same time. An analogous phonological correspondence occurs with the pronouns *quien, que, quienes,* and the adverbs *donde, cuando, como.* They are unstressed when in a merely declarative function, and stressed when their meaning is emphasized as determinative or interrogative forms.

Numeral adjectives exhibit a complex system of stress according to their position in the sentence. Although these modifications are mainly of a phonetic nature, their effect does not fail to reveal a clear-cut relationship with the meaning of the words.

The simple numerals, cardinal or ordinal, are always pronounced as stressed words. In the compound forms, the units and tens lose the accent when they are not in the last place: *dos mil, cuarenta y cinco*. *Ciento* and *cien* are exceptions, unstressed only before *mil*. The latter, in turn, always keeps the stress in any position whatever. *Uno, un,* and *una* do not lose the stress either, neither as numerals nor as indefinite articles. The plurals *unos, unas* are pronounced without stress in an approximate sense: *"unos veinte días."*

There exists in some regions the tendency to unstress the indefinite articles and the auxiliary forms *he, has, ha, hemos, han.* The same inclination is observed in *cada, antes, dentro,* and in other adverbs. No sufficient information is available on the geographic extent of these stress modifications so closely bound up with semantic evolution.

VIII.

Stress Groups

THE STRESS GROUP is formed by one or more words under a single breath accent. Vocables of secondary function, ordinarily unstressed, do not constitute a group by themselves. These vocables lean on the word that represents the principal element in the unity of each group. Every word corresponding to any of the species of first grammatical rank can constitute by itself one of these units. From the point of view of meaning, the stress group is the minimal fraction of speech with definite semantic value. At times these clusters are true melodic units, with individual function between the parts that make up the sentence. The modifications of the stress group affect in a direct manner the dynamic aspect of the pronunciation. The movement of these phonological units, with its impulses concentrated, extended, increasing, or decreasing, is the base on which the language depends for most of its stress effects.

The sentence is divided into phonic or melodic groups, with a pause or transition relatively marked between each other group. To perceive the accentual supports that determine the number of stress clusters included in each melodic unit is not difficult. But without the aid of the pauses or of the intonation inflections the line of separation between the stress groups does not always appear entirely clear. A considerable number of these groups consists of a single word, be it a noun, adjective, verb, adverb, or a stressed pronoun; but the units of this kind in which several words combine are much more frequent. The delimitation stands out distinctly when among the words of the group there is only one with stress accent: "El poeta—exhibe—su corazón—con la jactancia—del burgués—enriquecido—que ostenta—sus palacios." Antonio Machado. Doubtful cases are those in which next to the main word there is some other element without full stress but not quite unstressed either—a condition found specially in the auxiliary verbs, demonstrative adjectives, and indefinite articles: "El gusto—de la cortesía—y el cultivo—de las buenas formas,—freno—perpetuo—de la brutalidad—que hace vivir—a los hombres—en un delicado—sobresalto." Alfonso Reyes.

The length of these groups varies greatly. Besides the basic words, grammatical particles combine in them in the most diverse manner. Sometimes the group contains as many as eight syllables, and sometimes it includes only a simple monosyllable. The most frequent types are those of three, four, and five syllables. While some texts seem to prefer short forms, others show a certain inclination towards long combinations: *Cuando se lo dijo, por lo que se refiere, contra lo que se esperaba,* etc. The weak elements generally precede the stressed ones—which gives the stress line of the group a rising form, analogous to that presented by direct syllables and most words of more than three syllables. The enclitic position of the pronoun in some verbal forms, practically limited to the infinitive and imperative, *hablarle, dímelo,* occurs less than the proclitic, *me dijo, se lo dieron.*

The most frequent combination is that of preposition, article, and noun. Many pages of José Enrique Rodó, for example, register even more than twenty of these groups, like: *en la pluma, de la gracia, de la luz, a las almas, de una hora, en la paz, de la palabra, de una frase, de un pensamiento, de una imagen, para el alma, del niño, del regazo, en la voz, en el alma, a los párvulos, a los niños, de la imagen, sobre la idea, de la forma, de la verdad.* The kind of group made up of article and noun appears in second place. On the same page the preceding examples were taken from, the following ones appear too: *las cosas, el don, las ideas, la caridad, el beneficio, la sonrisa, el beso, el roce, la ternura, el artista, la verdad, el pan, la unión, la gracia,* and others. This form is followed by that of preposition and noun: *de abandono, de seda, de hadas, de misericordia, con gracia, a Dios, con pincel, con palabras, de armonía, en forma, con ritmo, en apariencias.* These groups are followed in smaller proportions by those constituted by pronoun and verb, preposition and verb, conjunction and noun, conjunction and verb, adjective and noun, and others.

Bisyllabic paroxytones constitute, as is well known, the most abundant lexical type in the language. The frequency of the groups of preposition, articles, and noun based on such paroxytones gives special prominence to the tetrasyllabic clause of trochaic rhythm. This effect is further enhanced by the paroxytones of four syllables, which, as has been seen, occur also in considerable proportion; by trisyllabic paroxytones preceded by a proclitic particle, *de camino, la ventana*; and by several other combinations fitting that same pattern, *de su mano, me lo dijo, se marchita,* and others. In short, this type of clause, which occupies first place among the stress groups, is the same element that serves as a basis for one of the rhythmic modalities more frequently used in octosyllabic verse:

> Vaquerito, —vaquerito,
> por la Santa—Trinidad,
> que me niegues—la mentira,
> y me digas—la verdad.

The analysis of the phonic group, as will be seen in the next chapter, confirms with new evidence the relation between phonological units of the spoken language and the constituent elements of popular verse. Based on the widely known trochaic rhythm, Spanish versification, in its most popular meter, uses as the predominant clause the type of stress group that occupies first place in the accentual and syntactic structure of the language.

IX.

Intonation Groups

THE DIVISION OF a text into melodic units is a task not always free from doubts and difficulties. The same text can yield a greater or lesser number of units according to the care or emphasis which is put on its reading. The melodic unit is the shortest portion of speech with a sense of its own and with a definite musical form. The boundaries of the melodic unit coincide with those of the phonic group. In the division of a text into melodic units circumstances of a logical and emotional order are influential. Emphasizing and evaluating the semantic elements of the sentence favors an increase in the melodic units. The feeling of measure or beat predominating in the rhythmic structure of every language has influence also as a special idiomatic element.[1]

It would seem that this mixture of influences could only give rise to discrepancies in the interpretation of any text read by different persons. However, experiments easy to perform demonstrate that such a division is much less free and arbitrary than is apparent at first sight. To be sure, absolute uniformity is not found even in the readings of a text repeated on different occasions by the same person. This depends considerably on the character of the text and the degree of clarity of its composition. In descriptive texts of a simple nature and even tone, the agreements and disagreements are usually of the same quantity and quality as are those that appear in the following selection from Azorin:

Estos tomitos | van adornados de estampas finas. Y en estas estampas, | vemos esos panoramas de ciudades | en que, por una ancha calle, | en una vasta plaza, | sólo se pasean o están parados | dos o tres habitantes. Muchas veces, | siendo niños, | y después en la edad madura, | hemos contemplado | en diversos libros del siglo dieciocho | y de principios del diecinueve | estas vistas de calles y plazas. En ellas, | nuestra atención, | nuestro interés, | han ido siempre | hacia esos tres o cuatro habitantes | que, ellos solos, | en la populosa ciudad, | gozan del vasto ámbito | de la plaza o la calle. Tienen una profunda atracción | estos solitarios personajes. A una hora del día | en que se supone que las calles y las plazas | están hirviendo de gente, | estos dos o tres habitantes | tienen para sí | toda la vastedad del espacio ciudadano.

All the persons asked to read this text aloud coincided in the divisions indicated. Some readers made also subdivisions within two or three of the groups seen above between lines. The results were surprisingly uniform considering the different possibilities of expression the text lends itself to.

These experiments were repeated on many other texts all of which can not be cited here for reasons of space. One of them was a selection from José Ortega y Gasset's *Meditaciones del Quijote*. The interpretation that rendered the greatest number of melodic units did not exceed seventy-five while the least did not go lower than sixty-six. In sixty-two of these divisions there was complete unanimity among all the readers. The instances of agreement corresponding to divisions of the text marked by orthographic signs—period, comma, semi-colon—were, in toto, forty. The rest of the divisions where there was agreement were produced without any orthographical indication.

It is evident that the sixty-two groups cited express the essential structure of the text in its phonological and semantic aspects. The details of form and content of the text itself make the basis for the uniformity observed in the division of its units. Long compound sentences of eight or ten groups were divided in identical manner by all the readers. The discrepancies recorded in other passages did not affect essential divisions but only certain groups that while considered as simple units by some individuals, were subdivided by others who perhaps gave a slower and more expressive tone to their reading. But in these same subdivisions there was also agreement and regularity among the few readers who made them. In the following reproduction of the aforementioned text, the divisions in which all the individuals concurred are indicated by vertical strokes, and by the letter 's' the secondary divisions made only in some of the readings.

> Al lado de gloriosos asuntos, | se habla muy frecuentemente en estas *Meditaciones* | de las cosas más nimias. Se atiende ˢ a detalles del paisaje español, | del modo de conversar de los labriegos, | del giro de las danzas ˢ y cantos populares, | de los colores y estilos | en el traje y en los utensilios, | de las peculiaridades del idioma, | y en general, | de las manifestaciones menudas | donde se revela la intimidad de una raza. Poniendo mucho cuidado | en no confundir lo grande y lo pequeño; | afirmando en todo momento | la necesidad de la jerarquía, | sin la cual el cosmos vuelve al caos, | considero de urgencia | que dirijamos también nuestra atención reflexiva, | nuestra meditación, | a lo que se halla cerca de nuestra persona. El hombre rinde el máximum de su capacidad | cuando adquiere la plena conciencia de sus circunstancias. Por ellas | comunica con el universo. ¡La circunstancia! | ¡Circum-stantia! | ¡Las cosas menudas | que están en nuestro próximo derredor! Muy cerca, | muy cerca de nosotros | levantan sus tácitas fisonomías | con un gesto de humildad y de anhelo, | como menesterosas ˢ de que aceptemos su ofrenda | y a la par avergonzadas | por la simplicidad aparente de su donativo. Y marchamos entre ellas, | ciegos para ellas, | proyectados hacia la conquista ˢ de lejanas ciudades esquemáticas. Pocas lecturas me han movido tanto | como esas historias ˢ donde el héroe avanza ˢ raudo y recto, | como un dardo, | hacia una meta gloriosa, | sin parar mientes ˢ que va a su vera ˢ con rostro humilde y suplicante | la doncella anónima que le ama en secreto, | llevando en su blanco cuerpo | un corazón que arde por él, | ascua amarilla y roja | donde en su honor se queman aromas. Quisiéramos hacer al héroe una señal | para que inclinara un momento su mirada | hacia aquella flor encendida

de pasión | que se alza a sus pies. Todos [s] en varia medida, |
somos héroes | y todos suscitamos en torno | humildes amores.
«Yo un luchador he sido | y esto quiere decir que he sido un
hombre», | prorrumpe Goethe. Somos héroes, | combatimos
siempre por algo lejano | y hollamos a nuestro paso [s] aromáticas
violas.

Contrasting with the relative uniformity of the division of
texts in ordinary reading, our attention is called to the great
differences that come up when those same texts are divided into
dictation groups. The following data referring to the above transcribed selection can serve as an example. The figures indicate
the number of groups into which the selection was divided in
reading and in dictation by some of the individuals on whom
these observations were made:

	Reading	Dictation
Subject A	68	91
Subject B	75	95
Subject C	71	98
Subject D	66	111
Subject E	68	120

Subjects like A and E, who in reading made the same number of units, showed nevertheless a difference of twenty-nine
groups when it came to dictation. The dictation had pauses in
all the points of division of the ordinary reading and in many
other intermediate places. Just as in reading the group division
is based mainly on the character and style of the text, in dictation, while still responding to this same influence, it follows
rather the manner of the person who dictates and the scale of
measure imposed by the greater or lesser facility of performance
shown by those to whom the dictation is directed.

Besides their logical basis, therefore, dictation groups, in general shorter and more numerous than those of intonation, are
influenced by the way and circumstances in which they are used.
As it is well known, the greatest fractionation in all cases is that
which results from the division of the text into stress groups.

The selection, whose maximum fractionation in reading and in dictation produced 75 and 120 groups respectively, contains no less than 137 nuclei of expiratory accent. Each one of these nuclei constitutes, as has been said, a portion of speech comprised by the action of a main stress. The significative and accentual individuality of the stress groups does not imply in any necessary manner the consideration of that same individuality in the melodic aspect. It may happen in certain cases that the stress group, the dictation, and the reading group will coincide among themselves; but ordinarily the latter is more extensive than the others. Frequently the phonic or reading group includes several stress nuclei which can more or less influence the tone movement without breaking the melodic unit of the group. It is not necessary for the tone movement to correspond to a simple and regular figure. The line of the melodic unit may present the most complex and varied forms between the two pauses, caesuras, drops, or transitions which bound its extent. One passes in many cases from one stress group to another without producing any of those effects that constitute the basis for the divisions in the melodic units. The stress group is an element with which one must count in the study of the intonation unit without considering it, at least in Spanish, as such a unit.

The delimiting of the melodic units of a text or a speech is indispensable to make the analysis of the corresponding intonation. The role of the intonation unit in speech is equivalent to that of verse in metric composition. The same essential elements which indicate the termination of the verse serve also as a basis for the division of the melodic units. From the combination of these units arises the melodic architecture of the sentence. The content of a text acquires concrete and definite value only when the form and the function corresponding to each one of its melodic units are established.

The length of the melodic unit is measured, as is that of the verse, by the number of syllables. It is obvious that spontaneous language proceeds here with great freedom. The series of units of any text whatever presents the greatest variety of measures without the slightest semblance of order and regularity in their length and combinations. The unit can be reduced to a simple monosyllable or be extended up to a high number of syllables. The count of such units in several passages of contemporary authors reveals, along with certain individual traits, a significant reservoir of common characteristics. The extent of the unit reaches even up to eighteen syllables in some authors. Actually measures of over fifteen or sixteen syllables are found only in negligible proportion. The mass of the scale is definitely constituted by units of five to ten syllables.

Considered as a whole, units of less than five syllables represent only 12.55% of the total and those of over ten syllables 19.54%, while those comprising between five and ten syllables add up to 67.60%. Within this area of greatest frequency, units of seven or eight syllables stand out specially. They alone make for 26.32%. From the standpoint of the differences existing in the authors examined, it can be observed that Ramón Pérez de Ayala and Gabriel Miró are the ones with a scale less extensive and more concentrated in the intermediate area. Miguel de Unamuno is noted by the use of long units. Groups of less than seven syllables represent 40.63% in Pérez de Ayala and 27.19% in Unamuno. Yet, groups larger than the aforementioned size reach 59.41% in Unamuno and 45.39% in Pérez de Ayala. Azorín (pen name of José Martínez-Ruiz), in spite of his known preference for simple sentences with few syntactical members, does not specially stand out for brevity in his intonation groups. Pío Baroja reveals a certain inclination towards groups consisting of between eight and fifteen syllables. The predominant group in Unamuno and Baroja is that of eight syllables, and in Azorín, Pérez de Ayala, and Miró, that of seven syllables. Juan Valera and Pérez Galdós have their most frequent measures in seven, eight, and nine syllables. Mariano José de Larra displays a shorter beat, five to eight syllables. Toreno (Conde de, José María Queipo de Llano), on the other hand, exhibits lengths of eight and nine syllables; and Marcelino Menéndez y Pelayo, going even farther, shows preference for those of eight, nine, ten, and eleven. Short lengths of less than five syllables, which in Larra represent 15.35%, in Valera and Galdós respectively do not exceed 9.92% and 8.54%, and in Toreno and Menéndez y Pelayo are reduced to 4.70% and 4.63%. On the other hand, long measures—above ten syllables—which in Larra, Valera, and Galdós amount to 15.00% approximately, in Toreno go up to 21.80% and in Menéndez y Pelayo to 30.40%. The latter, with units of sixteen and seventeen syllables, surpasses the figure that ordinarily serves as the limit for the other authors mentioned.

All the general characteristics described can also be seen in the writers of the Golden Age. The most common lengths waver between five and ten syllables. Fray Luis de León embodies his melodic groups in these lengths with a frequency even greater than shown in the previously cited texts. Units of seven and eight syllables constitute the main nucleus in the works of the Golden Age. And in general also those of five and six exceed those of nine and ten. The inclination toward short measures is quite noticeable in Saint Theresa and Cervantes. It shows above all in *Lazarillo*, where the most copious intonation groups are the ones of five and six syllables. In this same text the shortest measures, from one to four syllables, represent 22.45% as against 5.99% those between eleven and fourteen syllables. Francisco de Quevedo, in the exactingly overwrought style of his political and philosophical treatises, distributes his groups between the intermediate dimensions of five and nine syllables. Within this range, Quevedo places no special emphasis on any particular type of units. In his *Buscón*, where the language flows in a more lively and spontaneous way, measures of seven and eight syllables predominate considerably.

In texts of Fray Luis de Granada, Juan de Mariana, Baltasar Gracián, Diego Saavedra y Fajardo, and Antonio Solís the area of greatest frequency falls constantly also between five and ten syllables. Units of seven, eight, and nine are the ones that occur in the highest proportion within this range. The maximum extent of the intonation group does not usually exceed fourteen or fifteen syllables. Depending on the particular style of each author, the central nucleus of the units of seven, eight, and nine syllables raises or lowers its proportion, or shows a greater or lesser inclination either for the long or the short units. The axis

of the Mariana construction is the unit of eight syllables. It
shows as a whole remarkable symmetry and regularity. Also on
an octosyllabic base, the structures of Saavedra Fajardo and
Gracián display likewise balanced and symmetrical forms. Solís
shows lines more ample and vague, with manifest inclination
towards long measures. Gonzalo Céspedes y Meneses, in *El
español Gerardo*, has a marked preference for lengths of seven
and eleven syllables—as if the beat of his narration were influenced by the metrical preoccupation exhibited in the large number of poems inserted in the work.

The age and permanence of the phenomena revealed by these
facts is further confirmed when the experiments are carried over
to medieval texts. Medieval Spanish prose is particularly unanimous in the use of the length of eight syllables as the predominant unit. This first place, contrary to what has been seen in
modern classic texts, is rarely disputed by units of seven or nine.
The profile of the octosyllabic unit raises markedly above all the
others in the whole of the medieval texts. There is, however, a
manifest inclination toward the side of the short ones. Following the eight-syllable unit, the proportion of those of seven and
six exceeds considerably that of nine and ten. The total extent
of the scale is somewhat shorter than in the case of more modern texts. In Chancellor Pedro López de Ayala this scale is contained between three and thirteen syllables.

In the *Corbacho*, of Alfonso Martínez de Toledo, Arcipreste
de Talavera, the passages represented in popular speech display
shorter units than the rest of the work. This work coincides in
its general scheme with the other texts of its time in the predominance of the length of eight syllables and in the other characteristics mentioned as well. The passages in popular style
with their lively and rapid movement, raise the frequency of
the units of six and seven syllables over that of the octosyllabic
group, and in general reinforce considerably the proportion of
short lengths. In a mass of 539 groups of the *Corbacho*, those
of less than four syllables appear in a proportion of 15.12%
and those of more than ten syllables in one of 9.26%. Applied
to the *Celestina*, the same comparison gives 16.00% for the

short units and 7.86% for the long ones. Units of six or seven syllables appear with the same degree of frequency shown by those of eight. Data from *Lazarillo* and *Celestina* respectively reflect analogous proportions.

Ordinary conversation has a marked preference for short units. Naturally, the habit of speaking with greater or lesser rapidity makes a difference in every individual case. In general, standard Castilian elocution, even in current dialogue, is relatively grave. It does not usually group words in long units of hurried and fading pronunciation, as can be observed in certain modalities of Andalusian. In artistic expression in its most spontaneous form, the structural unit of Castilian is the octosyllabic group. Its measure and beat represent a certain degree of elevation over the style, more irregular and loose, of everyday dialogue. The inclination toward longer units than the octosyllables is seen only in the literary output of writers given to pompous elocution. At the same time, the tendency to shorter lengths is in some authors a stylistic device, while in others is the result of the influence of familiar speech.

It is evident that the grouping of words into melodic units follows the fundamental principles of the rhythmic tradition of the language. These principles are independent of the stylistic currents that have been influential in the longer or shorter grammatical extent of the sentence. Fray Luis de Granada's attempt to widen the scope of the sentence as well as Gracián's to condense thought into brief phrases have a common denominator in the analogous proportions of these melodic units on which the metrics of speech is founded. The difference between these two authors affects the syntactical organization of the words more than its rhythmic background. The result is a greater or lesser number of melodic units in the sentence. It is interesting to note that the texts of a more artistic quality, like, for example, those of Juan Manuel, Fray Luis de León, and Miró, are at the same time, because of the proportions of their measures, the ones that more closely follow the trends of the spoken language. These trends appear with more marked spontaneity in the works of *Lazarillo*, Santa Teresa, and Cervantes.

The differences become more noticeable when comparing the dimensions of the phonic group in several languages. Although scarce in number and measured by their respective publishers without a uniform criterion, some phonetic texts are available on which this comparison can be made. The French texts used for this experiment, in spite of having been classified by different authors, coincide in the distribution and proportion of their measures. None of the other languages examined has in this respect a range of action so small, nor emphasizes in such a marked way the dimensions of its predominant units. These units are distinguished by their extreme brevity. Such short measures are no doubt an instrument specially adequate to delimit and individualize even the smallest semantic nuclei of the sentence. The division of melodic units in French is based specially on the stress nucleus. Spanish ordinarily unites in one single melodic unit portions of speech that in French would make two or three distinct units. A. de Musset's text, which M. Grammont divides into 117 units in his *Traité de prononciation française,* would be reduced to approximately 70 if read with the normal standards of Spanish intonation. French measurements applied to Spanish, on the other hand, would give as a result a manner of elocution excessively cut up.

Spanish and English display characteristics quite similar in respect to the range of their intonation units and the proportion with which their preferred measures stand out from the whole. In both languages, the most extensive units rarely exceed fifteen syllables, the zone of greatest frequency being about the center of the respective series. English, however, tends more definitely to push that zone towards the short dimensions, situating it between four and eight syllables and causing those of six and seven to predominate. Spanish, as has been seen, insists particularly on units contained between five and ten syllables, with preference for those of seven and eight. Units of less than five syllables appear in Spanish with a proportion of 12.55% and in English with 22.27%, while those of more than ten syllables go in Spanish up to 19.48% and in English come down to 15.58%.

The largest measures concerning the extent of these units are found in German and Italian. Both languages present now and then groups of more than twenty syllables. Units over fifteen syllables, which in the French texts examined do not offer one single example and in Spanish and English represent only 1.23% and 2.27% respectively, appear in Italian in a proportion of 7.48% and in German of 7.22%. Faced with the divisions in Italian and German texts shown by these data, the Spanish reader feels himself inclined in many instances to subdivide certain groups whose disproportionate length contrasts with the melodic rhythm of Spanish. The measures appearing as predominant in Italian are those of six and seven syllables, just as in English; and in German those of seven and eight, as in Spanish. But the frequency proportion of these measures is in German and Italian considerably smaller than in Spanish and English. German and Italian distribute their groups throughout the whole scope of their broad scales without raising the outline of any of them with much prominence.

H. Klinghardt tried to discover the peculiar tendencies of each language on this particular aspect by asking people from different countries to translate the same text into their native tongue and divide it into melodic groups.[3] The text distributed by Klinghardt was so simple and empirical in its contents and form that it came out with approximately the same divisions in all the languages. All these facts show clearly the reality and nature of such tendencies. The delicacy and complexity of the matter, however, will no doubt require further investigations that will make these observations more precise. From this point of view, the three Romance languages—French, Spanish, and Italian—present a very different physiognomy. The sense of rhythmic clarity and of analytic precision implicit in the limitation of the unit scale of French and in the brevity of its predominant types contrasts with the amplitude and vagueness of the Italian measures. Between both extremes, the Spanish scheme occupies a place of tactful balance.

There can but exist a very close relation between the two roles that the group of eight syllables plays in Spanish as the basis of the phonological construction of the language and as the traditional and permanent primitive metrics of popular verse.[4]

The competition given the melodic unit of eight syllables by those of seven and nine seems also to reveal the basis for the alternation of the verses corresponding to such measures at a time when Spanish popular versification had not yet become fixed in its octosyllabic regularity. It is only natural that verses constructed under the influence of the metrical tendencies of the language should basically reflect the same essential measures that govern the division of speech into intonation groups. It is perhaps the cut down melodic units of French that have provided the model for the rhythmic clauses of one to five syllables of the most popular verse used in this language. In any case, neither this verse nor the Italian hendecasyllable can be considered as spontaneously influenced by the mentioned tendencies as the popular Spanish octosyllable—incarnation of the melodic unit predominant in the language, with no other complement than the minimal device of assonance.

The frequency proportion of the units of each scale decreases gradually from the predominant measures to those less used. It happens with the short units as well as with the long ones. These observations coincide essentially with the relation noted by Ramón Menéndez Pidal between the hemistichs of the *Cantar de Mío Cid* and other poems of irregular versification. The decrease occurs frequently alternating between the two kinds of units, just as in the aforementioned poems.[5] It is not, however, anything peculiar only to the old Spanish metrical system or to the phonology of the language. The order of gradual diminution seen in the measures that constitute the Spanish scale appears likewise in the scales of the other languages.

The same thing happens also with other kind of phenomena outside the linguistic field. In a comparison of the stature measurements of 100,000 military recruits of various origins it appeared that the greatest proportion, nearly 15%, corresponded to the height of 68 inches, with the rest of the heights, above and below, descending in perfect alternative regularity:

Predominant measure
68 inches: 14.91%

Smaller measures		Larger measures	
67:	13.21%	69:	14.00%
66:	10.24	70:	11.74
65:	6.81	71:	8.92
64:	4.06	72:	5.82
63:	2.11	73:	2.96
62:	1.12	74:	1.50
61:	0.49	75:	0.62
60:	0.26	76:	0.28

The statistical data about the weight of more than 200,000 persons show too the same kind of arrangement: a series of measures ordered like a pyramid whose top is the figure representing the most frequent weight and the sides the two scaled and descending lines of the larger and the smaller weights.[6] There is no question here that this is the natural order to which the manifestations of any oscillating movement caused by the inclination toward a given center must adjust themselves.

We have already seen how uniform the division of a text into melodic groups can come out as it is read by different individuals. The autophonic recordings of the Library of the Spoken Word of the Center of Historical Studies have provided the opportunity to confront the interpretation of the readers with that of the authors of the texts used themselves. In most of the cases, these recordings were made not from speeches or improvised talks but from written texts. Although the author may not always be the best interpreter of the artistic elements contained in his own work, his reading, nevertheless, constitutes material of prime interest for discovering the essential lines of the phonological scheme his writings correspond to. The authors of the recordings as well as the readers who were later asked to read the same texts, far from attempting to produce an artistic, more or less affected recitation, tried to adjust their reading to a form of expression natural and common. The divisions into melodic groups obtained from the readers were realized, to be sure, in independent experiments and while they were not yet acquainted with the original recordings of the respective authors.

In the recording of Baroja corresponding to his *Elogio sentimental del acordeón*, the text appears divided into ninety melodic groups. The reading of Baroja is quite rapid and fluent. Fourteen groups surpass the ordinary limit of fifteen syllables, but this does not prevent those of seven, eight, and nine syllables from making one third of the total. In the readings of the other persons, the number of groups fluctuated generally between ninety and ninety-five. Only one interpretation, done in a relatively grave tone, produced more than one hundred groups. All the pauses or caesuras made by the author, with the exception of four, were repeated in the same places by all the readers. Among eighty-six cases of agreement, twenty-seven correspond to orthographic signs representative of indispensable pauses, like the period, the colon, and the semicolon, and forty-five appear in places indicated by a comma. Some commas were unanimously treated as just signs without any value. The cases of divisions where there was agreement not indicated by any sign at all were fourteen. The only four cases in which the author had made divisions that did not come out in any other reading correspond to passages underlined by Baroja with a certain light emphasis. Such emphasis, understandable at the time of recording, may naturally be ignored in an ordinary reading.

Juan Ramón Jiménez distributed in fifty-nine intonation groups his prose recording entitled "Gusto. Belleza consciente." The calm and serene beat of his reading outlines with perfect clarity the form of each group as well as the highlights and nuances of each concept. By the play of its melodic measures, the text produces within its brevity an extraordinary variety of expression effects. The short groups, tense and concentrated, which constitute most of the recording, alternate with lengthy units of an undulating and tempered outline. The characteristics of this reading differ radically from those that mark ordinary narration. Many of the divisions of the text are of course indicated by orthography; but even those not expressly called upon by written signs were made with surprising regularity in the various readings subsequently compared with the author's recording. The discrepancies refer to delicate nuances like one that can be observed in the following example. Here is how the written text goes: "de ellos es de donde debieras ir cayendo, blandamente, como de una suave ladera." Most of the readers, led by the commas that isolate the adverb *blandamente*, read: "de ellos es—de donde debieras ir cayendo—blandamente—como de una suave ladera." The author, however, ignoring the orthographic guideline, had joined in a single group *cayendo blandamente*, following no doubt the indivisible relation with which both concepts were probably associated in his mind. And surely to make this image even more definite and clear, separated it from the verb *ir*, whose meaning also acquires this way a more individualized and independent value: "de ellos es—de donde debieras ir—cayendo blandamente—como de una suave ladera."

Among the seventy-five groups counted in the recording of Ramón del Valle-Inclán, consisting of a selection from *Sonata de otoño*, half are over ten syllables and some exceed double this length. The most frequent units are distributed within a wide zone comprising between five and fifteen syllables. The melodic movement of this recording offers an extraordinary variety of musical effects that show in the extensive scale of its intonation groups. All the readings compared coincided in reflecting this same quality. In all of them, long groups appeared in large proportion, following the essential characteristics of the author's reading.

In the analysis of more extensive selections of this same work of Valle-Inclán, the pattern that emerges from the proportion of their measures does not correspond exactly to the regularity and symmetry of the picture obtained from other texts. Besides the broad scope in which their turns of phrase develop, it can be said that no definite measure acts as their predominant support. Preeminence corresponds in a certain way to the hendecasyllable, with a metric structure more or less regular.

The rhythmic background of the prose of Valle-Inclán is made

of the Galician combination of dactylic and trochaic clauses—
as E. Martínez Torner has justly observed in *Música* journal,
Barcelona, 1938, fascicle III, page 10 and following. This internal, subconscious rhythm is clearly evidenced not only in the
lyric prose of the *Sonatas*, but also in works of a different character and atmosphere like those included in the series of *Ruedo
Ibérico* and even in *Tirano Banderas* itself. A single page of this
novel shows the presence of this rhythm in several passages,
witness the following: "El ministro de España—apoyando el pie
en el estribo—diseñaba su pensamiento—con claras palabras
mentales." "El Barón, maquinalmente,—se llevó la mano al sombrero.—Luego pensó:—Me han saludado." "Que me destinen
al Centro de Africa—donde no haya Colonia Española."

In the vernacular dialogue of the characters of *Tirano Banderas*, this same rhythm appears frequently: "¡Qué voz de cor-
neja sacaste!—¡Yo no niego la vida del alma!"—"De no haber
estado tan bruja,—hubiera guardado este día." "Si me pusieses
en un pupilaje,—ibas a ver una fiel esclava."

On the basis of this movement, whose metric beat is constituted by the indicated combination, the number of syllables of
the verse or of the melodic group comes to be a secondary element in Valle-Inclán. The epic rhythm, trochaic and of more
primary and simple features (studied by Gili Gaya in the journal *Madrid*, Barcelona, 1938, fascicle III, pages 59–63), tends
evidently to organize in Spanish in units of eight syllables. In
both cases, melodic divisions occupy in the composition of the
discourse definite places made manifest by the sense and the
style of each text, even though in many cases there is no visible
mark to indicate them. As he constructs his phrases and sentences in the manner adequate to the demands of his thoughts
and emotions, the author keeps setting the extent and limits of
these units as an indispensable complement to the expressive
function of the words. The text receives and permanently con-
serves this intimate phonological architecture upon which an
essential part of its meaning and character depends. The reader,
on his part, perceives the existence of such divisions. They define and specify the phonetic and semantic contour of each word
in the uniform progression of the written line.

X.

Phonology of the Sentence

ORDINARY CONVERSATION UNFOLDS in general in short sentences, with a marked predominance of those of a single group. In the dialogues in the plays of Jacinto Benavente, the Alvarez Quintero brothers, and Florencio Sánchez, sentences of a single group represent more than half of each text, and those of two groups, about one fourth. Those of three and four groups descend gradually to lower figures. The dialogues of novels, with greater freedom of elaboration, introduce extended sentences in greater proportion than it is the case in dramatic works.[1]

The structure of the sentence becomes more varied and complex in oral dissertation, and reaches its maximum extension in speeches. The lecturer and the teacher utilize relatively extensive sentences in which circumstantial and complementary elements entwine and cause the number of phonic groups to increase. There must be small difference between the syntactic forms of the academic explanation and those of the written language. The tone of the elocution influences the extent of the sentences in a manner analogous to the influence it exerts on groups. The form of the reasoning depends in large part, as is known, on the subject treated and on the occasion it is spoken. But there is no question that in this respect there are also common habits whose proportions serve as a basis for certain modes of speaking or of writing to appear as made up of long or short sentences.

The analysis of several narrative selections—not dialogue— of Pérez Galdós shows that sentences of four, five, and six groups are the ones that constitute the body of the prose of this writer. Shorter constructions, of one, two, or three groups, and longer ones, of seven, eight, or nine groups, appear as a whole with less frequency. Sentences of ten or more groups are hardly found in Galdós, except in the inexcusable multiplication of members of enumerative series.

In the narrations of Valera sentences of over six groups appear usually in predominant proportion. Those consisting of between ten and fifteen groups surpass in some passages even the number of shorter constructions. Similar results are found on examining some selections of José María Pereda. The extension not only of the sentences but also of the phonic groups is in Valera and Pereda somewhat longer than in Galdós. In Emilia Pardo Bazán and Palacio Valdés the predominant measures are more similar to those of Galdós than to those of Valera and Pereda.

The combinations of the sentence in the descriptive pages of Baroja give visible superiority to the types of two, three, or four groups. The extension of the phonic group, as well as that of the sentence, tends also in this author to short measures. Sentences of two, three, and four groups predominate likewise in Valle-Inclán, Azorín, and Miró. Nevertheless, in these same writers special cases are found of long constructions with a high number of such units. It has been noted elsewhere that the length of the phonic group is in Miró shorter than in Unamuno and Baroja. As for Valle-Inclán, there is in him a visible inclination towards lengthening the aforementioned groups. The differences in length of units combine with the other elements that, within the common basis of the abbreviation of the sentences, constitute the personal accent of each one of these authors.

José Martí and Rodó cultivated in general the sentence of ample expression, in which the high and tense level of the elocution calls for numerous and prolonged groups. In the speeches, manifestoes, articles, and letters of Martí the variety of tones is greater than in the writings of Rodó. More than half of the sentences in the dissertations of the great Uruguayan essayist contain from five to ten phonic groups. The rest are distributed, with a notable effect of harmony, between short sentences of less than five units and dense constructions which include at times more than fifteen long groups.

The bold sentence, of a brief and polished cut, is abundantly cultivated in Spanish America among contemporary writers. In Eduardo Barrios, sentences of more than five groups are rarely found. Alfonso Reyes presents a greater variety and freedom; but the phonological basis of his elocution is also constituted by sentences of two, three, or four groups. On the same base is the style of Ricardo Güiraldes constructed, in *Don Segundo Sombra* as well as in *Xaimaca*. The length of the groups in these authors, within their dependence on the basic measurements of the language, does not fail to tend likewise toward short types.

The literary language has developed in every epoch some aspect of sentence construction. Phonological and syntactical transformation have come together, although the lines of each of them may not correspond completely. In the old prose, sentences are grouped in long paragraphs, with the tenuous and repeated linking of a few conjunctive particles. A living reflection of this tradition seems to be preserved in the narration of popular stories. Sentences of two, three, and four groups, with a simplicity of coordination similar to that of the old texts, form practically the whole of these narrations. The Renaissance language adapted classical expressions, gave more amplitude to the sentences and showed how to put flexibility and harmony in the junction of words. Romantic style added extent and rotundity. The modern tone prefers the agile sentence, of varied form and moderate extent.

Numerous examples confirm the observation made elsewhere about the distribution of the phonic groups into the two parts, protasis and apodosis, in which the sentence is divided. The first part of the sentence is usually, in effect, shorter than the second. This heightens and condenses the appellative function of the anticadence. In sentences of three groups, the most frequent distribution places one group in the protasis and two in the apodosis: "Por toda su obra posterior—hay un vago susto—de que el corazón se le ahogue." Reyes. Among those of four groups, the prevailing form does not distribute the units symmetrically but rather assigns a single group to the protasis: "Para distraer el susto,—salto de la cama—y finjo sorpresa—ante el paisaje que Peñalva me señala." Güiraldes. The same contrast appears repeatedly in longer sentences, even when the protasis may be formed by two or more units: "Más tarde,—acrecido el tumulto de la revolución,—rotos los frenos de la tribuna pública,—surgen aquí y allá—los periodistas valientes,—los portavoces del pensamiento nuevo,—luchadores que usan de su pluma—como de algo vivo y cotidiano." Reyes.

The enlargement of the first part of the sentence is probably employed in certain cases as a mere modification favorable to the harmony and variety of the period. It is more common, however, to find this enlargement in cases in which the slowness of the elocution appears to correspond with the character and style of the text being read. In the writings of Azorín, for example, the sentences of this type are much more abundant than in those of Baroja. In the cases of sentences of three groups, Baroja employs especially the usual combination 1–2, while Azorín uses in great proportion the form 2–1. Constructions hardly used by Baroja, in which the groups are distributed in the ratio of 3–2, 4–3, 5–2, etc., are relatively frequent in the passages in which Azorín describes the peaceful environment of Spanish towns: "En la sala grande, que encontramos a la derecha, conforme entramos, aparece un cañizo con una manta." "Las campanas de los franciscanos, de los agustinos, de los dominicos, de los mercenarios, de los capuchinos, de los trinitarios, están llamando a misa."

XI.

Spanish Accent

THE MOST PREVALENT ideas in popular opinion in regard to the character of any language concern the peculiarities of the accent more than any other aspect of the spoken word. Outside of those persons who for special reasons can talk concretely about definite characteristics of grammar, lexicon, or pronunciation, what people think in most cases about any language arises essentially from the impression of the accent.[1]

By virtue of this impression, every language takes in the mind of the people a unique physiognomy, with qualities more or less pleasing and adequate. Because of their accent, languages seem clear or obscure, smooth or harsh, monotonous or musical; some prove to be flexible and delicate, others uncultured and rude; some are admired and praised, and others are considered lacking in beauty and attractiveness.

The image we have of a living language is above all an acoustic image. The characteristics that compound this image match the phonetic effects perceived in the language. Naturally, there can not be such a representation of a language that one knows only in its written form. Dead languages are nothing but languages without an accent, mute tongues that speak with the signs of writing, without timbre or quality of voice.

A living language is like a sonorous instrument: it has a definite acoustic character. Depending on the dexterity and inspiration of the player, the instrument will sound with more or less fluency, freedom, and facility; but always with its own timbre.

It is the timbre or quality of a language or dialect that we call accent. Or by more familiar names, tone or inflection.*

The accent is made up not only by the musical ingredients these names bring to mind, but by the total effect that results from the diverse phonetic elements of the language in its habitual dynamics. That is to say, by the manner in which these elements come about and combine, independently of their semantic function, voluntary and conscious in the act of expression.

Factors of the accent are the individual shade of the sounds within the phonological type each one represents; the relative frequency with which the various sounds are employed in the current usage of the language; the more or less rapid or slow tempo or beat of the diction; the degree of the expiratory intensity where it does not affect the particular phonology of the word; and the musical movement of the voice, outside of its role in the logical and psychological actualization or determination of each phrase.

To study the accent of a language is to search for the secret of its phonetic nature, which is the basis of its social characterization and the prime and permanent cause of many of its dialectal differences, as well as of most of the transformations occuring throughout its historic evolution.[2]

The definitive formula of the accent of any language has not yet been stated. Phonetics, up to now, has been occupied primarily with the individual study of articulated sounds within the narrow field of the isolated vocable. Works devoted to the study of the phonetic mechanism of the language in the phrase and in the discourse are few. The cadence analysis begun by Professor Edward Sievers and the phonological works of the Linguistic Circle of Prague are modern endeavors to focus attention on this field. Unfortunately, the means now available for an objective and experimental investigation are still far from possessing the necessary perfection that the delicacy and complexity of the subject require.

Nobody is unaware, however, of the fact that each language

* Translator's note: The Spanish is *tonillo o dejo.*

has its own accent and its own different manner of sound. We perceive immediately the accent of people whose mode of speaking is different from ours. The one accent we know less is the one we ourselves use. It is as difficult to perceive the accent of one's native tongue as it is to appreciate the timbre of one's own voice.

The idea many people have that Spanish is spoken without accent or intonation of any kind is altogether wrong. The Spanish accent is as evident to the French ear, for example, as the French to the Spanish. The accent is the most authentic sign that lets us discover the nature of a person. Likewise, it is the first thing that declares and defines us before others.

It is quite understandable that the idea one has of the accent of a foreign language, considering the subjective nature of these impressions, is influenced by the euphonic habits one has been accustomed to by the orthoëpy of his own language. It is also just as possible—bringing over to the linguistic field impressions of another character—that the idea of the accent of a given language is influenced by attitudes of like or dislike arising from the kind of political relations existing between one country and the other. At any rate, it seems that not much importance should be attributed to such influences. Notwithstanding certain discrepancies of secondary value, people from different countries and languages recognize and judge in a similar way the essential qualities of the accent of a language. What the Spaniard A. de Eximeno said about the musical richness of Italian, its lively and varied inflections, and its overflowing sonority coincides with what has been observed about this same language by French, English, Danish, and other writers.[3] As for Spanish, as we shall see later, coincident opinions have been likewise expressed by the most diverse people.

Because of their individual acoustic qualities, the sounds of the language and the combinations made with them produce in our ear different impressions. In fact, the aesthetics of the articulated sound could be considered part of the musical aesthetics. It was not an arbitrary invention of poetical symbolism to assign to each vowel or consonant a definite aptitude for expression.

Aristotle used to recommend to poets to take into special account the innate value of the sounds of language. Juan de la Cueva, Francisco Cascales, and many others among the Spanish, even in very recent books, have made on this point particular observations whose comparison with each other would be interesting.

As a natural effect of this quality of sound, words possess, together with their historical value, the expressive quality that corresponds to their phonetic composition. In onomatopoeic words both elements conform to each other. But the acoustic value of the words plays this expressive role even in cases where this correspondence does not occur. In a certain way, every word has always something of onomatopoeia about it. Even if we think that we are paying attention only to their ideologic meaning, words make us perceive at the same time the sense implicit in their voiced structure.

The standard ordinary fabric of the inflections of tone, the expiratory force, and the beat of the elocution completes the effect of the sounds in what concerns the expressiveness of the phonetic shape of the words—or, as has been said, the evocative magic of their musical essence. It is true that on such slippery ground one can easily fall into the nonsense of acrobatic linguistics—a disorder that Pérez de Ayala portrayed admirably in the ingenious figure of his Belarmino. It behooves modern phonology to study methodically these facts, exaggerated at times and ordinarily ignored. It is upon their undeniable reality that the concept of each language's accent achieves in substance general unanimity, regardless of the circumstantial differences that may influence its evaluation.

The languages whose accents they use to talk more frequently about in Spain—aside from what is said about the Hispanic languages and dialects themselves—are French, Italian, English, and German. Italian is considered musical, harmonious, and vehement; French is praised for its conversable, refined, and flexible form; English seems dull, hissing, and imprecise; and German is judged rough and hard.

Popular tradition has given picturesque forms to these impressions. A good example is the old saying attributed to Charles V, already in circulation in the seventeenth century, according to which English is the language to speak to birds, Italian to compliment ladies, French to converse with men, and Spanish to address God.[4] A well-known epigram of don Juan de Iriarte describes too the characteristic image of the accent of several languages. In English it is the whistling; in Italian the sigh; Spanish is called harmonious song; and French is represented by its aptness for conversation.[5]

Unamuno, speaking about insular English, used to call it sea whisper. As for German, it is usually characterized in these and other similar references by its crudity—just as Emperor Julian had done centuries before commenting on the war songs of the primitive Germans.

The essential lines of these impressions are further reflected in the passage in which Madame de Staël alluded to Rousseau's saying that the languages of the south of Europe are daughters of taste while those of the north of necessity. She noted that, in effect, Italian and Spanish are well modulated as harmonious singing; that French is eminently adequate for conversation; that English, on account of the parliamentary exercise and the natural energy of the people, has a certain expressive gift that makes up for the prosody of the language; and that German, much more philosophic than Italian, more poetic and daring than French, and more ductile than English to the rhythm of verse, keeps nevertheless a certain harshness. This impression of German was due to the little social and public cultivation this language had had up to the time when the cited author was writing.[6]

As regards Spanish, what is really the character of its accent? What features distinguish it among the accents of other languages? Are we Spaniards in a position to define the composition of our own accent and judge impartially in the matter of its aesthetic qualities?

Every language is pleasing, sweet, and harmonious to those who speak it as their native tongue. The words of the most

abrupt accent sound euphonically to the ears of those who
learned them from their mothers' lips. To the native speakers
of a language its words awaken many echoes besides those
which arise particularly from the acoustic effect of the sounds.
In *Persiles y Sigismunda*, when the lost adventurers, after days
of anguish, arrive at a coast where they hear Spanish spoken,
one of them exclaims with great emotion: "Since heaven has
brought us to a place where the sweet language of my country
sounds in my ears, I almost consider certain the end of my mis-
fortunes." (Book I, chap. XI.)

Among the praises the Spanish language has received on different occasions from some of our writers, rarely do they allude
specifically to the qualities of its accent. Generally, such praises
are founded on patriotic sentiments, on historical considera-
tions, and on political or cultural aspirations rather than on the
special appreciation of the nature and resources of the language
itself.[7] The most enthusiastic modern apologies for the language
come from the pen of Spanish-American writers. Because of the
many factors that stimulate or restrain these attitudes, the fact
is that the love for the language—which in the sixteenth century
was a general sentiment and that even in the eighteenth inspired
comparisons and parallels with other languages—is displayed
today in Spanish America with greater vitality than in Spain
and not only in the literary and grammatical fields but in the
current commentary of everyday subjects as well.[8] But although
we may share in the fervor and enthusiasm of these praises and
admire moreover the eloquence with which many of them have
been written, we must recognize that the virtues they extol cannot be shown to be unique with Spanish. Who will not find in
his own language, as Juan Pablo Forner praised in ours, majesty
for great things, simplicity for ordinary things, tenderness for
amorous things, etc.?

The statements of Spanish Americans and Spaniards are of
special interest for our purpose when they refer to the effect the
peculiar way of speaking of each group produces on the other.
Worthwhile recording in this connection is the passage in which

the Argentine Juan B. Alberdi tells how, living in Madrid and staying with families of that town, "more than once the speech of the children and the ladies distracted me from music itself on account of the harmony of its accentuation."[9] A similar impression can be found among the lively and original passages of Domingo F. Sarmiento: "The Spanish women have in Spain a decided advantage over the natives of Spanish America, not only in the pronunciation of the *ce, ci,* which they perform so sweetly and effortlessly, but in the resolute manner of speaking so genial in this tongue. A ¡*mire usted*! in the mouth of a Spanish woman from Castile is priceless."[10] Also worthy of mention is the statement another Argentine, E. S. Zeballos, makes about Dr. Miguel Navarro Viola, a member of his country's Congress: "I still hear his vibrant voice and his pronunciation worthy of Valladolid, exclaiming in mid-debate: "Mr. President, let our language be spoken! Let our laws be written in Castilian!"[11]

It is in foreign writers where the most interesting and instructive information and the opinions we can consider most impartial on the character of the Spanish accent are to be found. Many are the writers, professors, and travelers from different countries who have talked about the effect that hearing the Spanish tongue has had on them. The image of our way of expression, something we cannot appreciate ourselves, comes to us reflected from the ear of people of other languages.

Most of the comments of these people coincide in pointing out in the Spanish accent three principal characteristics: sonority, a manly air, and a tone of dignity.

Concerning the first of these characteristics, *The Edinburgh Review* (1841) said that the Spanish language, because of its richness, sonority, and flexibility, is in itself like a kind of free verse.[12] George S. Hillard, an American, tells how at a meeting held in Rome (1850) at which as many as sixty different languages were spoken, Spanish stood out among all of them by its sonority and prosodic beauty.[13] The Swedish philologist, F. Wullf, wrote that in his opinion the Spanish language is the most sonorous, harmonious, elegant, and expressive of all

the Romanic languages.[14] Going even farther, the Englishman
G. Borrow said that Spanish is the most sonorous of all the
existing languages.[15]

The reason for this quality lies no doubt in the character of
the Spanish vowels and, particularly, in that of the variants of
these same vowels most frequently used by the language. The
timbre of the more often used vowels determines the predominant shade in the color of the accent.

Spanish, as we have seen before, uses mainly the vowels *a*,
e, *o*. It has neither mixed nor properly relaxed vowels. It does
not maintain either, as do other languages, as marked differences between long and short vowels or between open and close
variants of the same vowel. Nasalization, which attenuates and
obscures the sound of the vowel, does not have in Spanish the
spread and degree it has in Portuguese and French. The vocalic
series of Spanish is the clearest and most simple of the European
languages. The euphonic instinct of Castile, rejecting vague and
unsteady forms and defining very early its prosodic preferences
(possibly under influences of the most remote origin), worked
up a firm and transparent vowel system. And not only is this
system the basis of the sonority foreigners admire in Spanish,
but also, as Menéndez Pidal has said, it constitutes the foundation of the surprising uniformity with which Spanish maintains
its phonetic unity in all the countries where it is spoken.[16]

Miguel Antonio Caro notes how Isaac Vossio (1618–1689),
observing the frequency with which Spanish repeats the vowel
a and the finals in *o*, attributed to the influence of these sounds
the impression of sonority and gravity this language produces.[17]
The famous Giovanni J. Casanova, who considered Spanish one
of the most beautiful and sonorous languages in the world,
thought too that the source of these qualities lay in the abundance of *a*'s—which he called the queen of letters.[18] Surely Edgar Quinet referred to the effect of the vowels in balanced syllabic articulation when he alluded to the speech of the women of
Madrid, remembering their words like a rain of pearls on a
fountain.[19]

As for the manly character of the Spanish accent, numerous

references are likewise found in foreign writers. The observation appears repeatedly in them that the phonetic contexture of this accent makes it at once energetic and suave, dense and flexible, soft without being bland, and vigorous without being hard. In the combination of these qualities Waldo Frank saw one of the aspects of the equation of balance in which he considers the powers of the Spanish soul concentrate.[20]

Spanish and Italian are often subject to comparison on this point. Spanish is recognized to possess a stronger and more pronounced architecture. For the French grammarian L. Malefille, Italian seems to have inherited specially the sweetness of Latin, leaving the nerve to Spanish. Italian, he says, is the daughter of Latin; Spanish its son.[21]

This same impression was already common among our Golden Age writers. Fernando de Herrera said that the Spanish language "in the ease and softness of its pronunciation should be treated with more honor and reverence; Tuscan with more delicacy and simplicity." Bernardo de Aldrete remarked that "if we look for suavity and sweetness, Spanish has it, accompanied by great genius and majesty appropriate to real manly character."

The impression of strength of the Spanish accent comes no doubt from the relative volume and prominence that the prosodic stress has in this language. In French the individual accent of the words is diminished and effaced under the sentence stress. Italian puts emphasis on the words with a rising tone more than with an increase of intensity. In Spanish the stressed syllable of each word brings about along the line of utterance a support from the expiratory effort. This support will be greater or lesser according to the emotional impulse with which the word is pronounced. In short, the stress accent proves to be in Spanish visibly stronger than in Italian and more regular and frequent than in French.

The organs that produce and regulate the modifications of stress are located in the thoracic cavity. The manly character that the use of this stress gives to Spanish results from the activity that its nature and mechanism demand from that center of the body. The tension and energy where the emphasis of the expression originates French puts mainly in the mouth, Italian in the throat, and Spanish in the chest. It has been rightly observed that Spanish must be spoken with fullness and candor, filling up with vital breath the ample volume of the words.[22]

Reduced to the proportion corresponding to feminine speech, this quality is present too in the manner of speaking of the Spanish woman; although the intensity here, instead of being projected outwards in the elocution, is rather transformed into density and amplitude of the internal resonances.

The danger of expiratory energy consists in the facility with which it can lead to forms of excessive violence in passionate elocution. Referring to the famous speech in which Emperor Charles V challenged Francis I before Pope Paul III, the Frenchman Pierre de Branthôme said that if the Emperor on that occasion used Spanish instead of the customary Latin, it must have been, among other reasons, because the Spanish language possesses qualities specially suited to bravado and threats.[23]

The regularity and prominence of the expiratory force, in effect, lends to Spanish pronunciation a certain firmness that contrasts with the flexible and vague line of French accentuation. Benito Feijoo noted rightly the influence of education on the predominance and degree of the force with which the language distinguishes its stressed syllables, "Spaniards there are who articulate with great suavity, and I do believe that almost all men of some politeness do it thus." In any case, if he had had to choose one way over another, Feijoo declared that his preference would have gone for the Spanish accent—"because a manly prowess is a more noble talent in a language than an effeminate softness."[24]

Such prosodic characteristic, often represented with extreme exaggeration, has also been arbitrarily explained by saying that Spanish, because of habits of domination and authority acquired through centuries of conquests and political imperialism, employs as its ordinary and current mode of expression the exclamation, the shout, and the command. This statement, in the preface of a collection of texts of Nebrija, Juan de Valdés, Fray Luis de León, Ambrosio de Morales, and other writers of the sixteenth and seventeenth centuries, happens to be totally incongruous. These texts, models of thoughtful and discursive style, and the numerous references that reflect the continence and restraint people noticed in Spanish manners in those times, roundly contradict the opinion of the collector we have alluded to.[25]

Branthôme, with more tact and correctness, limited himself to pointing out the aptness of Spanish for authoritarian and imperative expression, but without considering this its usual and peculiar mode. The impetus of the expiratory accent can give rise, in effect, to those brusque and violent discharges that Pereda liked at times to put in the mouth of some of his characters, constructing these expressions with vigorous plasticity. In a passage of *Sotileza*, the voice of Carpia, being heard suddenly from the rear of the hall, threw Gilda, says Pereda, to the farthest corner of the bedroom, as if it actually had the force of a catapult. In *La Puchera*, Berrugo is the one who usually speaks with that energy: "Doña Inesita and doña . . . who? asked don Baltasar, with a force of stress on the *who* that was felt by don Elías in his kidneys, just as if Berrugo had pierced him through that part with the prongs of a pitchfork."

Expressions of violence in environments of a low cultural level come out more or less the same way in all languages. Abrupt speech is a universal sign of a crude nature. The relative intensity that gives the Spanish accent its manly temper is far from such excess. The feature of this accent more unanimously recognized in the allusions of foreigners is not so much sonority or energy as dignity—a characteristic incompatible anyhow with any disproportion or excess in the expressive resources of the spoken word.

One author says that Spanish, with its nobility and dignity, exercises a powerful attraction on the mind and the ear;[26] another adds that the harmony and majesty of this language surprises and delights travelers from the north;[27] still another finds justification in these qualities alone for what has been said about the Spanish language being the most adequate one for speaking with God.[28] It should be sufficient to cite these notes of illustrious professors from New York, Cambridge, and Brussels, among other similar references. After this, it may not appear excessive for a Spanish-American author to have written with satisfaction that the sole fact of speaking in Spanish does by itself give exalted lineage to the speech.[29]

Just as the sonority is primarily based on the timbre of the vowels, and the virile firmness on expiratory intensity, the nobility and the dignity observed in the Spanish accent have intonation as their phonetic basis. The Norwegian linguist John Storm, the author of notable phonetic studies on various languages, made a comparison of Spanish and Italian intonation. He noted that while the latter, with its lively and ample undulations, runs through the whole musical scale, Spanish cadence, more uniform, severe, and restrained, concentrates on precise and not so numerous forms.[30]

Extending the comparison to French, the same author added in another passage that for an ear specially accustomed to the prosody of the Germanic languages, French intonation ordinarily proves to be somewhat high, delicate, and feminine. Italian exhibits a richer, more complete, and varied register with more ample intervals than French. Italian intonation produces a certain impression of vehemence; the French is more properly refined. Spanish, on its part, is more serious, dignified, manly, and martial, and employs more sharply defined intervals than the other Romance languages.[31]

The musical cadence of Spanish, especially in Castile, is, in effect, relatively low and solemn. Italian and French are spoken, in general, in a higher tone and with a more rapid rhythm than Spanish. On speaking Italian or French, the person accustomed to Spanish feels impelled to raise the line of the voice above its habitual tone. Frenchmen and Italians experience the opposite on speaking Spanish.

In the melodic movement of conversation or of discourse, Spanish does not develop rising and repeated scales as French, or amply undulated expressions as Italian, or falling inflections as English, or broken and angular lines as German. Spanish puts the tone at the height corresponding to each melodic group, and sustains it, as in balance, at the same level approximately within the body of the group. Spanish intonation is not composed of scales, arpeggios, or ligatures, but of prolonged notes, relatively uniform and harmonized with each other by regular intervals. The order and beat of these movements and the purity and sobriety of these lines give the Spanish accent its solemn harmony and its lordly distinction.

One can understand that such qualities, added to the noted prominence of the expiratory intensity, have given the Spanish accent a certain martial air. Storm observed it, as has been seen, in the passage cited above, and, among others, it was noticed also by Longfellow, who said that in spite of its prosodic suavity, Spanish resounds like martial music.[32] A poet of the West Indies has called Spanish the language of golden verses and martial vibration.[33]

On the other hand, the uniform and insistent notes of Spanish intonation, its long strokes, its clear inflections, and its solemn rhythm lend themselves in a special way to a style of grandiloquence and pomp. When the melodic elements of the language are stretched out beyond their ordinary proportion, martiality turns into arrogance, dignity into emphasis, and composure and decorum into majesty.

In *Exequias*, of Forner, the Spaniard Arcadio noted complacently how among the various peoples inhabiting Parnassus our compatriots were distinguished by the pomp and pageantry of their accent.[34] With analogous satisfaction, maestro F. A. Barbieri took notice that a French writer had called Spanish, on account of its prosodic richness and pomp, the language of orators.[35] A. W. von Schlegel said that Spanish is a sonorous, light, and fluid language with ample and majestic musical periods that delightfully caress the ear.[36] Quinet saw in Spanish the melody of Italian, the roughness of Arabic, the vigor of Saxon, and the grace of Provençal. These qualities all added to majesty, which was, in his judgement, the peculiar and unique characteristic of Spanish itself.[37] Somerset Maugham puts in the words of one of his characters a eulogy of the lordly nobility of Spanish. With image similar to that employed by

Dominique Bouhours, this character remarks that the impression one receives of Spanish is comparable not to the murmur of the brook but rather to the low rumble of the overflowing river.[38]

Hillard, the American already mentioned, considered Spanish admirably suited for grand occasions and elevated thoughts: "a manner of expression," he said, "appropriate for kings and ambassadors." But for this same reason it seemed to him that Spanish could not yield with flexibility and simplicity to the ordinary dealings of everyday life. The Swede Wulff, on his part, thought that the Spanish language, alongside of its sonority, harmony, and elegance, possesses a kind of solemn and pompous affectation that at times becomes tiring.[39]

There is little doubt that foreigners as well as Spaniards have referred on this particular point to special features of the language that do not justly reflect the real quality of the Spanish accent. In ordinary and current speech Spanish does not have the solemnity and majesty noted by the preceding quotations. On the other hand, on the stage, in the pulpits, at assemblies and congresses, and at the habitual occasions of political campaigning, one does find abundant examples of emphatic language. Not many are the people who having to speak at a public function succeed in expressing themselves with simplicity and naturalness. People known for the plainness of their conversation adopt an affected and solemn air when it comes to making a speech.

One of the greatest difficulties for stage directors in show business is that of avoiding affected declamation. Cervantes, listing in *Pedro de Urdemalas* the qualities of a good actor, warned, among other things, that he should be "not affected in gestures nor should he deliver his speech putting on airs."[40] From behind his retable, Maese Pedro advised his servant to be simple, on seeing him become grandiloquent in his narration. Modern plays include at times instructions from the authors recommending the performers to avoid a solemn and declamatory tone.[41] The stamp of the ham actor has remained as the proverbial type of emphasis. Grandiloquence and pomposity, in short, do not occur in Spanish as ordinary and peculiar characteristics of the accent, but rather as conventional forms of an artistic tradition whose propensities found, naturally, fertile ground in the phonetic qualities of the language.[42]

The feature given as the main characteristic of Spanish in several foreign references is its harmony. The most recent evidence in this sense appears in a grammar for the teaching of Spanish in Romania. In its preface the illustrious professor N. Iorga declares that Spanish is the most harmonious of the modern languages.[43] The foundation of this characteristic is not, as G. Mayáns believed, the fact that Spanish words are regularly long and lack complicated groups of consonants;[44] or the proportionate combination of consonants and vowels, as Antonio de Capmany said;[45] or how variably placed the accents may be in the words, as it is said in the Grammar of the Academy.[46] Any one of these particular circumstances can be found, almost in the same manner, in several other languages, specially those of the Romance family, just as in Spanish. The harmony of Spanish consists of a total effect made up by the proportionate combination of the clear and complete timbre of the vowels, the medial temper of the consonants, the regular movement of the expiratory intensity, and the solemn, sober, and even stream of the musical inflections of the voice.

It should be noticed that the manner of speech these opinions we have been commenting on refer to is, specially, that of the Castilian provinces. One author mentions this expressly and restricts his observations to the qualities present in Spanish prosody as heard from the people of the same region that gave the language its name.[47] The accents of the other Hispanic regions and lands display, in their multiple varieties, other characteristics and suggest other impressions.

In the Andalusian accent, in a general way and specially in its Sevillian modality, the articulation is softer than in Castilian, the expiratory intensity weaker, the rhythm more rapid, and the tone higher. The melodic expressions of Andalusian are agile, flexible, and lively; they rise in delicate scales up to relatively high notes and they fall harmoniously with grace and suavity. This liveliness and grace of the Andalusian speech becomes particularly elegant and sparkling in feminine mouths. Cristóbal Suárez de Figueroa, in *El Pasajero*, praised with effusive words the voice and the pronunciation of the women of Seville.[48] Just as it is said of the Galician woman that she seems to coo when she speaks, the manner of speaking of the Andalusian woman is compared rather to the warbling of birds. Of the *Goletera* of Arturo Reyes, for example, it is said that she spoke as if she had a lark in her throat. The speech and the laughter of the miller's wife in *El sombrero de tres picos*, modeled on the Andalusian image, sounded like the pealing of the bells on Holy Saturday.

Among all peninsular accents, Galician is distinguished by its slow rhythm and its melodious softness. Its most tranquil, harmonious, and song-like modalities are heard in the villages of the Galician mountains. The Galician vowel system has closer and more obscure shades than the Castilian, although in lesser degree than Portuguese. The basis of Galician articulation, intermediate between the Castilian and Portuguese, tends towards the rear of the oral cavity, which contributes to the bland, temperate, and lyric effect of the sounds. Its most prominent melodic feature consists in the frequent repetition of a movement of the voice in which the tone, beginning the phrase or the phonic group on a relatively high note, descends with a smooth and waving inflection on the following syllables. F. Navarro Ledesma, emphasizing the gentleness and suavity of this accent, said of Xan, the sentimental Galician of his *Egloga*, that he could not even giddap his mule. He did it with so much indulgence and in such a sweet tone that the poor animal fell asleep.[49]

Catalan accent shows a robust and full prosodic effect. Clear sounds stand out among its vowels, in spite of the abundance of the neutral and dull sound of its unstressed, *a*'s and *e*'s. Its consonants are in general articulated with firmness and precision. Just the opposite of Portuguese, which is interiorly articulated with the jaws almost closed, Catalan is pronounced with a powerful resonance of wide opening of the mouth.

Catalan and Valencian surpass Portuguese and Galician in sonority. Portuguese and Galician are superior to Catalan and Valencian in gentleness and suavity. The tension of its final consonants give a kind of hardness to Catalan, as do also the relative force of its expiratory impulse and the impetus of its intonation. The Valencian Eximeno said that Catalan pronunciation is sonorous and well modulated, but a bit rough and coarse.[50] Coinciding with this same impression, it has been said in a more literary guise that the nature of Catalan appears in its ballad, which bears the smell of the mountain pines with the tar of the pirate ships and the salt of the sea.[51]

Spanish-American accents show very diverse forms in regard to the pronunciation of certain sounds, and specially in the modalities of rhythm and musical cadence. The attenuation of the expiratory force on which the peculiar vigor of the speech of Castile rests is a general feature of the Spanish of America. It seems that in its stages of geographic expansion, from Old Castile to New Castile, Andalusia, and America, Castilian was gradually reduced in the force of its original intensity. Adaptation to the conditions of each area and the evolution of social relations between the dates in which each new modality was developed was, without doubt, the cause of such modification. A major influence on the current idea in Spain concerning the Spanish-American accent seems to have been the impression of West Indian speech. In general, it is attributed to it a soft and lazy slowness, a sweetness and languor that even in the West Indies corresponds not so much to the speech of the mountain peasants as to that of the coasts and the plains, where there are many colored people. Pedro Henríquez Ureña has noted the difference between the high tone and vivacious tempo of Havana and the low tone and andante tempo of Santo Domingo.[52] From one country to another there are variations in the articulatory tension, the level of the normal tone, the amplitude of the melodic inflections, and the tempo of the elocution. Those who have been exposed to the different impressions of Spanish-American speech will remember among the multitude of its variants the refined modulation of the Ecuadorian of Quito; the repeated scales, gradually rising, of the Argentine intonation of Jujuy; the sustained lines, high and uniform with rhythmical final drops, of the Venezuelan of Caracas; and the syncopated Puerto Rican, strewn with frequent and rapid high inflections.[53]

What can be the origin of this diversity of accents? How within the same language have these cadences, drops, and accents, which so clearly allow us to distinguish Castilians, Aragonese, Andalusians, Argentines, Chileans, Mexicans, etc. come to be?

Not only each country or region, but each individual has in his manner of speaking a personal and unmistakable stamp. The most significant element of an individual accent is the timbre of the voice. By his voice the old and blind Isaac recognized his son Jacob, even though by his hands he confused him with Esau. Mary Magdalene recognized the beloved voice of Jesus in the garden of the holy sepulcher when the day of resurrection dawned. One who changes his clothes and covers his face so as not to be recognized does not really disguise himself unless he alters his voice. In this sense there are improper stage situations, like that of the Laurel Inn of *Don Juan Tenorio*, in which don Diego Tenorio speaks to his son in his natural voice and the latter does not recognize him only for the simple fact of seeing him covered with a light mask.

While in the theater and in novels friends and relatives may often speak to each other without being recognized, people can recognize by his voice the neighbor who speaks on the street or the one who knocks at his door at night. On a certain occasion, the press published news of a woman who had recognized the announcer of a far-off radio station by his voice as her son who had disappeared from home many years before. The impression of the voice is deep and lasting; many memories are erased before the remembrance of the voice.

The individual accent, in the shades of the timbre, tone, and intensity of the voice and of the speech, reflects particular psycho-physiological conditions and inseparably accompanies each person, both when speaking his own language and when using a foreign tongue. The idiomatic accent, on the other hand, consists of external forms established as collective habits, whose adoption, unconscious or purposeful, classifies us with the tone and style of a definite linguistic community.

Among the phonetic characteristics that compose our manner of expression, some correspond to the social medium in which we have grown up, while others are the effect of our own nature and characterize and distinguish us above the prosodic background of the idiomatic common accent.

The infinite variety of oral expression, considered in individuals of all countries and languages, may be reduced, according to Ottmar Rutz, to four cardinal types. To the first, whose psycho-physiological manifestations are characterized by a rounded form, a circular turn, and a soft, obscure, and melodious voice, belong principally the Italians, Polish, South Slavs, and Romanians. The second, of oblong forms and turns, eliptic, with a soft and clear voice and of sober and measured melody, is that of the Germans, Austrians, Swiss, English, and Dutch. The third type, of triangular forms and broken lines, with a clear and metallic voice and with cadences more rhythmic than melodious, is the Greek, Celtic, and Semitic manner; it predominates among the French and Spaniards, although influenced in these peoples by the first and second types of Romans, Germans, and Anglo-Saxons. The fourth type, of mixed and shapeless outlines and with a hard and obscure voice, seems to be represented mainly by the black peoples of Africa.[54]

Within this venturesome classification, whose principles have merited the acceptance of recognized psychologists and linguists, O. Rutz finds an intimate correspondence between the characteristics of the oral expression and the form, movement, and attitudes of the body. On account of the geometric characters displayed in these phenomena, the first of these types has been called spherical, the second parabolic, the third pyramidal, and the fourth polygonal. With proofs all too brief and not quite convincing, Rutz maintains that fray Luis de León belonged to the pure or moderate pyramidal type and Calderón to the warm pyramidal type.

The affinity of conditions of temperament and character, and the influence of similar circumstances from the physical and social environment give rise to collective phonetic habits that differentiate the accent of each country or region from that of other groups of the same generic type. In the way of shaping the form of the words, in the tendency that guides the modification and selection of sounds in the making of a phonetic system, and in the rhythmic and melodious configuration of the line of speech, each people gives preference to the modalities that best conform to the expression of its character. One, as for example, French, carefully carves and polishes sounds, syllables, and inflections; another, such as the English, carries out the articulations and movements of speech in a vague, imprecise, and relaxed manner; another, as the Italian, exerts itself in the external projection of phonetic phenomena in clear and sonorous forms; and still others, like Portuguese, lean towards a muffled pronunciation, with suave and temperate interior resonances.

Whether the intonation uses certain inflections, or the vowels are pronounced with greater or lesser clarity, or the expiratory force acts with more or less energy, or the tempo of the speech is hastened or slowed down are points that, alongside of habits inherited by oral tradition, are influenced continually by the peculiar reactions of individual idiosyncrasy and inclination. In substance, the phonological structure of a language is the product of the contributions of all the people who throughout time have been leaving the anonymous traces of their temperaments and preferences on the patterns of common speech. Accent is, in this sense, that aspect of language through which each people reflects most authentically its mode of being. Words can have varied origins; accent belongs to the proclivities of the psyche and to the inheritance everyone collects in the land where he grows up.

The idiomatic accent, once established as social norm, prevails within its province over individual tendencies, and imposes itself even on people of a background different from that which originally made it a manner of expression. Accent, like the other habits, forms, and materials of a language, is inherited.

Nevertheless, a person may speak other languages besides his own native tongue and give to each its proper accent, yet maintaining at the same time in all of them the peculiar characteristics of his individual expression. To pass from one accent to another is to change prosodic base in order to be situated in the proper atmosphere of the other language—an indispensable condition for entering its intimacy and that of the people who speak it.

Eça de Queiroz used to say that a man should not try to speak with assurance and purity any but the language of his own country. All the others he should speak badly, proud of speaking them badly, with a foreign accent. For it is in language where nationality truly resides, and one who would be possessing with increasing perfection the languages of Europe, would be gradually undergoing denationalization.[55]

Although Eça de Queiroz directed his irony specially against affected eagerness to pronounce foreign languages correctly, his advice has not failed to be taken seriously by some professors. But, why not see the same sin of correct pronunciation also in the other aspects of language? Does it not denationalize also to speak a foreign language with correct vocabulary and with grammatical purity? Far from this, the truth is that the better one knows other languages, the more the mastery of one's own is refined and strengthened. The incorrect use of a foreign language simply denotes ineptitude or lack of preparation, not at all brilliant qualities with which to honor the nationality one belongs to. Respect for the foreign language as well as the aptness and efficacy of its use oblige us to accept it just as it is, without corrupting it with words or improper expressions or deforming it with strange pronunciations.

The impression of the accent of a people is inseparable from the idea one has of the character of that same people. Because of this Ch. Bally finds occasion here for some groundless attributions. He says in this respect that German passes in France as a rough and unharmonious language, while Spanish enjoys a much different reputation in spite of possessing many of the phonetic asperities of German.[56] The harshnesses to which Bally refers, without pointing them out concretely, cannot be other than the sound of the Spanish *j*, analogous to that of the German *ch*, and perhaps the contrast of the stress accent, more pronounced in Spanish and German than in French. The frequency of the *j* is in German about five times greater than in Spanish. Other harshnesses of German, like the joining of complicated groups of consonants, an aspirated and voiceless release of the sounds *p*, *t*, *k*, and specially the very frequent hard attack or striking of the glotis in word-initial vowels, are unknown to Spanish.

In any case, the roughness or harmony of an accent does not depend on the effect of this or that detail, but on the symphonic totality of its various elements, and in this sense it cannot be surprising that Spanish and German produce a different euphonic impression, although they coincide in some of their phonetic traits. With the same prosodic elements different accents are formed, just as different melodies are produced with the same notes of the musical scale.

Character, as a permanent emotional source of ordinary everyday expression, shapes the accent, and the accent molds and depicts in sound the image of character. It is not without basis, therefore, that each one is indistinctly attributed the qualities of the other.

Foreigners are usually impressed by the seriousness and dignity they find in general in the conduct of Spanish people, even when they belong to the most humble classes. There is hardly a book about Spain in which there is no mention of the villager who wraps himself in his cloak with aristocratic elegance, of the peasant who rides on his donkey with the distinction of a knight, or of the beggar who extends his hand with a lordly air.

As opposed to the excessive loquacity of the playboy and the city worker, the Spanish peasant is ordinarily sober of speech and solemn and sententious in his expression. This is the way Chisco, the strapping young workman of *Peñas Arriba*, was,

better at fighting bears on the mountain than at relating his
deeds; and the old man Tomba of *La Barraca*, who at each meeting with the gardener Batiste repeated to him as a foreteller of
doom: "Believe me, my son, they will bring you misfortune";
and the Cordovan Matapalos of *La Feria de los discretos*, a master at the art of bringing up an engaging and sly remark while
calmly rolling a cigarette.

Eximeno observed that a Spaniard, on beginning a sentence,
manages the intonation as if he were going to sing; but immediately, in order not to depart from gravity, he usually proceeds
in an unvaried key. The normal effect of the Spanish accent is,
in fact, to show a certain restrained vehemence, a certain repressed energy. All this gives it a relatively tense expression and
does not let it go into turns or inflections of excessive amplitude.

It has already been noted how this accent is sonorous because
of the quality of its vowels, manly because of the proportion of
its intensity, and dignified because of its intonation cadences. It
may be added that its rhythm is firm and calm like the meter of
the popular ballad, and its tones sober and warm like the colors
of Velázquez.

Many of the observations commented upon indicate that the
qualities perceived in the Spanish accent do not refer solely to
the present-day language. The serious and manly dignity,
pointed out by contemporary writers, was noted in the same
way by Eximeno in the eighteenth century, by Bernardo de
Aldrete in the seventeenth, and by Herrera in the sixteenth. How
long has the Spanish accent been presenting this character? Did
it acquire its martial air and noble bearing from the influence the
discoveries and conquests of the sixteenth century might have
had on the national spirit? Could the Spanish accent have been
different before those events?

Menéndez Pidal has given us two valuable pieces of testimony
concerning the euphonic effect of medieval Spanish.[57] One of
them is that of the Arabic writer Ben Hayyan, who on describing how the count of Castile, Sancho García (995–1017), was
dressed in the Moslem manner and seated on large cushions in
his traveling tent while dealing with notables of the Moorish

city of Tudela, expressed his admiration for the dignity, nobility, and persuasive elegance of the Castilian leader's manner of speech. Another is the passage of the poem of the Conquest of Almería, of the middle of the seventeenth century, in which the poet, a Leonese monk probably, alluded to Castilian prosody comparing it to the clear and martial sound of trumpets and the drum: "*illorum lingua resonat quasi tympano tuba.*" According to these ancient reports, Spanish had already its dignified, martial, and virile air almost a thousand years ago, when it hardly began to be used as a written language.

The dignity and the decorum of the Spanish accent show in many of the sketches of gentlemen of the fifteenth century written by Hernando del Pulgar. We know, for example, about Iñigo López de Mendoza, the Marqués de Santillana, that "in the moderation of his appearance and in the soundness of his speech bore himself like a generous and magnanimous man." About don Juan Pacheco, the Marqués de Villena, and don Pedro Fernández de Velasco, the Count of Haro, we are told that they spoke with much grace and with reasoning that everybody heard with pleasure. King Ferdinand the Catholic, friendly and communicative, spoke in a calm and measured tone. "He had a manner of speaking," says Pulgar, "neither hurried nor too deliberate." About several other gentlemen we read too that it was their custom to speak soberly, without prolixity. A distinguished example we have in the bishop of Avila, don Alfonso de Madrigal, "a silent man in whom the light of knowledge showed more than the flashiness of speech."[58]

In all these sketches emerges that "*gravità riposata*" that Baltasar Castiglione praised in the Spanish character. It surely manifested itself not only in the attitude and the gesture, but specially in the manner of speaking.[59] The style of the speech of Don Quixote exhibits too these same features, with no other difference than a more prominent display in the aspects of intonation, repose, and gravity.

We do not know if the tone and accent with which we read today the *Crónica General*, the *Conde Lucanor*, or *La Celestina* are the same that guided the prosodic feeling of their authors when they wrote these works. But we believe we sense inwardly a perfect correspondence between the phonological impression of such works and the tone, rhythm, and beat of the Spanish we speak today.

Eduard Sievers affirms that each text reflects and preserves in its passages the peculiar prosodic modality of the author who composed it, and that a spontaneous reading awakens and revives at any time the sound waves implied in the written words.[60]

This statement rings with a note of truth. Its confirmation would provide a new and important resource for literary and philological criticism. Unfortunately, no scientifically practicable way has been discovered up to date to penetrate the sphere of these cadences of the accent, which lay asleep in the lines of text as the notes in the strings of the harp or as the bird in the branch.[61]

The forms and styles of the accent do not fall within the domain of linguistic consciousness. They are not functional elements, like the phonemes, or the words, or the semantic inflections of intonation. This very unconscious and incorporeal character tells us that they are indeed habits singularly resistant. Contrary to what M. Weingart suggests, it does not seem at all to be the case that the significance of the accent of a language is bound to the atmosphere and circumstances of each epoch—no matter if, in effect, each epoch and even each generation can be distinguished by some modality or peculiar shade within the same common and permanent background.[62] It can be observed, moreover, that the idea of each accent is maintained in essence in the opinions about foreign languages, even though political relations between the respective countries may have varied a great deal from one epoch to the next. The idea of the permanence of the accent is the basis of Sievers' doctrine of the cadence analysis. He believes to have found reflected in German medieval texts certain melodic distinctions which even today are heard in different parts of Germany.

Everybody knows that in speaking a foreign language nothing resists so much giving up and allowing itself to be replaced as the accent of the mother tongue. In place of the words, combinations, and expressions of the native language, we learn to use the corresponding forms of the foreign one. But we do not succeed, except at the cost of great effort, in concealing the accentual habits we unconsciously practice and replacing them by those of the language we are trying to speak.

In bilingual regions the national language is commonly spoken with the accent peculiar to each region. If the national language succeeds in gaining ground in these regions, it does so really in the areas of vocabulary and grammar, but not in that of the accent itself. One may say that more than to the language itself the accent belongs to the people who have originated it. The accent is not in the letters, or in the words, or in the sentences, but in the manner of saying them. Within a same language, different accents are used among different countries or regions. The language changes accent when it spreads and passes from one country to another. People, on the contrary, go from one language to another without changing accent. The identity of accent presupposes ethnic ties closer than the identity of language. The boundaries of the accents represent the most subtle and profound frontiers of the social geography of a country.

The accent with which Castilian is spoken by the peoples of Aragon, most of them made linguistically uniform centuries ago by the influence of that language, is probably the same with which they spoke their ancient Aragonese dialect before adopting the tongue of Castile. The Aragonese people speak generally with a clear articulation, with a tone relatively slow and deep, and with a marked intensity that imprints a certain roughness on the frank and noble effect of the expression. The Ansotano and Cheso dialects, remains of the Aragonese dialect preserved in hidden valleys of the Pyrenees, coincide essentially in their prosodic character with the peculiar accent of the rest of the region. The most characteristic trait of this accent consists of the relatively high tone with which the sentences ordinarily end, even though they are not interrogative. In analogous circumstances, the final inflection of a normal statement ends in Aragonese on a note six or eight semitones higher than in Spanish.

Outside Aragon, this form of intonation is found also in the Basque provinces and in Navarre. Menéndez Pidal, studying Aragonese toponymy, discovered an abundant primitive fund with Basque characteristics.[63] J. Saroïhandy, likewise, thought the treatment certain sounds receive in Aragonese dialect to be vestiges of a linguistic past in close relationship with that of the Basque language.[64] The Aragonese language, attached to the land and resistent to all influences, is, perhaps, the most vivid and eloquent evidence of this tradition.

Even concerning facts so particular and concrete as, for example, the confusion of the *s* and the *z* in the pronunciation of many Andalusians, it has been proved that such confusion had existed in Andalusia for several centuries. Furthermore, there are reasons to believe that it had existed there already long before the first known testimonies.[65] And if a phenomenon of this nature shows such persistence and duration, what age would we have to presume for the rhythm and cadence characteristic of the Andalusian accent?

An example of my own experience is that of the island of Puerto Rico, where English was introduced with the American domination. The English spoken in Puerto Rico is pronounced with the same Puerto Rican accent as Spanish. If Spanish should one day disappear from that island—a not very probable contingency—the Puerto Rican accent would survive in the English that would be spoken there. The Puerto Rican accent may have originated as a result of the mixture of different manners of speaking in the Spaniards from different provinces who came to reside on the island. Although more probably it comes from the prosodic cadence that the native population used in their indigenous tongue and continued using in Spanish.

The Spanish language came to America with its philological material and its cultural substance; but the majority of the Spanish-American accents are probably the inheritors of indigenous cadences. This question could be clarified by the study of the accents of Mexico, Peru, and Paraguay, for example, in comparison respectively to those of Náhuatl, Quechua, and Guaraní, tongues still spoken by part of the population of those countries.

As for Mexico, Henríquez Ureña says that the intonation of the popular classes is identical to the one they show when speaking Náhuatl—an influence observed also, although in a more attenuated degree, among the educated classes.

The heritage of the accent bears witness to the collective continuity of a definite psycho-physiological attitude and of the oral forms corresponding to its expression. The Spanish accent, purified and refined throughout many generations, can be considered in its essential traits as the oldest traditional element of the language, prior probably to Castilian Romance itself. It is the millenial echo of the verbal styles of all the peoples who have preceded us in the land where we came into the world and in which our mode of existence has taken shape.

Literary Phonology

XII.

Mío Cid

FOR THE STUDY of the phonemes in the *Cantar de Mío Cid* the first hundred and the last hundred verses of the poem have been taken into account. The count has been made on the critical text of R. Menéndez Pidal, Madrid, 1908. The first hundred verses yield 3,119 sounds and the last hundred 3,184. The same gross similarity that these figures show is observed in the particular comparison of the phonetic elements that enter into the composition of the passages cited. It does not seem adventurous to extend to the entirety of the work the phonological character resulting from the examination of these 6,303 sounds. These data could be of help in trying to discover what Spanish must have been phonologically in its first literary manifestations.

The total of the simple vowels, with exclusion of the diphthongs, amounts in the *Cantar* to 42.59%. In classic Latin the proportion of the vowels was 38.48%. The reduction many Latin words suffered in Spanish, at the cost specially of the consonants, undoubtedly made the proportion of the vowels rise. Modern Spanish, under cultural influences, has favored anew the inclination towards the Latin order. The proportion of each vowel in Latin, in the *Cantar*, and in the present-day language is seen in the following figures:

	a	e	i	o	u
Latin	6.94%	10.74%	9.82%	6.70%	4.28%
Cantar	14.41	11.36	3.89	11.70	1.23
Mod. Span.	13.00	11.75	4.76	8.90	1.92

The most frequent vowels in Latin were the *e* and the *i*. The *a* appeared to a markedly lesser degree, as did the *o* and the *u*. The sum of *a, o, u* gave a figure smaller than that made by the *e* and the *i*. The predominance of these two vowels, with their palatal and high timbre, must have influenced Latin acoustics in a considerable manner.

In the *Cantar* the *a* came up to first place with the high proportion of 14.41%. The *e* and the *o* remained in second place with very similar proportions. The *i* and the *u*, losing a great deal of the frequency they had in Latin, came out below the other vowels and some consonants. While the *i* lost in Spanish 5.93% with respect to its original measurement, the *a* gained 7.91% and the *o*, 5.00%. With the situation thus inverted, the sum of the palatal vowels *e, i* came to be in the *Cantar* almost half of the figure represented by *a, o, u*. The frequency of *a* and *o*, which by themselves alone constituted more than a fourth of the total of the sounds, would put a solid and solemn stamp on the language of the poem.

The verses of the *Cantar* in which the *a* occupies the strong syllable of the rhyme constitute 56.33% of the totality of the poem. Those in which the said syllable is occupied by the vowel *o* represent 39.30%. Not less than 95.63% of the syllables that play the most important role in the sonorous line of the verse corresponds throughout the entire length of the poem to the vowels *a, o*, with an advantage of 17.03% in favor of the first. The insistence of the *a* within and at the end of the verse stands out in numerous cases:

"Inchámoslas d'arena ca bien serán pesadas" line 86.
"Al padre e a la madre las manos les besavan" line 2607.
"Espada tiene en mano mas no la ensayava" line 3662.

In discussing the frequency of the sounds, it was pointed out how Spanish, by the fact of raising the proportion of the vowel *a* to the first place of the phonological scale, departed from the Latin tradition and came to coincide with the example of Basque. The increase of this phoneme in Spanish is not the result, as one might think, of the fact that feminine nouns are more frequent than masculine ones. Remember the information given on this point on page 49. Neither can this be explained sufficiently by the fact that there are many words of Arabic origin in which the vowel in question abounds. There are entire pages in which not a single word of that origin appears without this fact causing the *a* to descend from its pre-eminent place. Its greater phonetic resistance with respect to the other vowels and the great number of verbs to which the prefix *ad* or *a* attached itself—at times without any visible specific function: *adobar, adornar, amasar, asaltar*, etc.—must have contributed no doubt to emphasize the prominence of this sound.

It is natural that the transformation or loss that the, *a* has undergone in French under diverse influences, and the peculiar form of the feminine plural in Italian have reduced its proportion in these languages. The phonetic and morphological circumstances in which such changes have taken place could be pointed out; but the need will remain anyway to explain the causes that have given rise in this and so many other cases to the fact that the same original materials have been treated in each country in a different way. There must have been some reason—which in this case should not be sought in the vague areas of the least effort nor in the influences of climate—why Spanish should be from the beginning so determined to maintain, reinforce, and multiply this clear and sonorous vowel instead of submitting it to the changes and reductions it has experienced in other languages.

The repetition of the *o* in the *Cantar* is much the result of the frequency with which there appear in the narration preterits of the type of *arrancó, dexó, besó,* and oxytones like *señor, varón, sabor, Campeador*. The assonance that this type of words represents is the most frequent among all the combinations used by the poem at the end of the lines. Outside of the rhyme, the *o* is repeated also in numerous cases with marked insistence:

> "De todo conducho bien los ovo bastidos" line 68.
> "Fincó los inojos ante todo el pueblo" line 1318.
> "El rey don Alfonso essora los llamó" line 1895.

After the acute rhyme in *ó*, used in thirty series with 1,453 verses, one finds in the poem in order of frequency the following types of assonance: *á*, 884 verses in thirty-nine series; *á–o*, 675 in thirty; *á–a*, 542 in twenty-nine; *í–a*, 61 in eight; *í–o*, 44 in six; *í*, 18 in two; *é–a*, 11 in three; *e–o*, 11 in two; *ó–a*, 8 in two; *ó–o*, 5 in one. In all, the rhymes with tonic *á*, *á*, *á–o*, *á–a*, amount to 2,101 verses, with a great advantage over those 1,466 verses having assonances in tonic *ó* represented almost in their entirety by the acute type.[1] The four types *ó*, *á*, *á–o*, *á–a* comprise 3,554 verses of the 3,730 which the poem contains. The combinations with stressed *é* and *í* are rare, and types formed on the basis of the *u* are lacking altogether. With more or less frequency, the *Cantar* utilizes eleven of the twenty assonances the language possesses.

In the old ballads the most usual assonances are *á–a*, *á–o*, *í–a*. Among the 890 ballads of the first volume of the *Romancero* of Agustín Durán, the assonance *á–a* reaches the proportion of 25.84%, *á–o* 23.59%, *í–a* 13.48%. These are followed with less representation by *é–a* 8.08%, *á–e* 6.05%, *é–o* 3.82%, *í–o* 3.50%. The acute assonances in *a*, 3.50%, and in *o*, 2.58%, are not found in the ballads with the frequency they have in the *Cantar*. The narrative imperfect of the ballads makes its assonances with infinitives and preterits less frequent than in the assonances of *Mío Cid*. The principal source of the three most frequent assonances in the ballads are the imperfects and the participles. After *é–e*, 2.58%, and *o–e*, 1.23%, the rest of the combinations appear in very small frequencies. The only assonance of which no example is found among the ballads cited is that of acute *u*.

In the verses examined from *Mío Cid*, we find the rising diphthongs, *ia, ie, io, ua, ue, ui, uo*, and the falling ones, *ai, ei*. The most repeated, as in the present-day language, are *ie, ue, io, ia*. The cases with this kind of phonemes are after all so few that adding up all the types found in the mentioned verses they do not exceed the proportion of 2.66%. *Ei* appears only with two examples and *ai* with one. To this same falling form belong the diphthongs *au, eu, oi, ou*, of which there was no case. Neither was there any example of *iu*.

The voiceless stops show quite similar percentages: *p*, 2.31%; *t*, 2.80%; *k*, 3.76%. Among the voiced ones, the *d*, 5.74%, stands out alongside of *b*, 1.47%, and *g*, 1.43%. Besides, *v* appears with 1.69%. It seems that the sounds corresponding to *b* and *v* must have been as little differentiated in the old speech as the stop and fricative varieties with which they are heard in the modern pronunciation. The sum of both sounds in the poem surpasses the percentage of the *p*, although not with the advantage which the *d* shows with respect to the *t*. Learned and technical words of the modern language have considerably raised the proportion of the phonemes *p*, *t*, *k*.

After the vowels *a*, *o*, *e*, the most frequent phonemes are the consonants *s*, 7.59%, *l*, 7.41%, *n*, 7.41%, and *r*, 5.46%. Only the *l* is more frequent as syllable-initial than as final. As for the *s* and the *n*, the final position makes up almost two-thirds of the figures indicated for each type. The difference is less marked between the initial, medial, and final *r* (*moro*, *prado*, *corte*), although in this case also the last position is the most repeated. The *m*, for the most part initial, drops to the proportion of 2.41%.

The frequency of the voiced *s* of *fermosa*, *guisa* does not exceed 0.37%. The addition of this fraction to the figure of the voiceless *s* reaches a level approximating the one this phoneme shows in contemporary Spanish. Consonants of rare appearance are the *ç*, 1.50%, the *z*, 0.55%, and the *f*, 0.66%. In spite of the reduction the *f* had to undergo at the time when it was aspirated and then dropped, the learned words in which it appears have caused its proportion in the modern language to be higher than that displayed in the texts prior to the time of its transformation.

The old language possessed, as is well-known, an extensive series of palatal phonemes. Nevertheless, the most frequent, represented by *g*, *j*, did not exceed the proportion of 0.65%. The percentages of the remaining ones were *ll* 0.40%, *ch* 0.36%, *ñ* 0.38%, *x* 0.22%, and *y* 0.22%. The proportion corresponding to the whole group, although small, 2.23%, was greater than that which the palatals *ch*, *ll*, *ñ*, *y* amount to in present-day Spanish.

The type of syllables recorded in the first hundred verses of the poem and the proportion of each type appear in the following table. The hiatus in *seer, veer, engrameó, rey, criador, mío,* has been taken into account in the syllabic delimitation; synalepha has been adopted in *grado a tí, me an vuolto, a la exida;* and liaison between final consonant and initial vowel has been applied: *estás en alto, por Burgos aguijava:*

ba	48.50%
bab	28.14
a	11.99
ab	6.88
bba	3.35
bbab	0.88
babb	0.13
bbabb	0.13
	100.00

The types *ba* and *bab* predominate also in Latin. The examples corresponding to the forms *babb* and *bbabb* are limited to the words *Alfons* and *grant*. Hiatus and the repetition of the copulative *e* must play a principal role in the relatively high showing of the type *a*, which in modern Spanish only amounts to 5.07%.

The phonological structure of the words is concentrated intensely in bisyllabic paroxytones. Their proportion surpasses by more than seven percent that which this kind of words possesses in the present-day language. In the high proportion stressed monosyllables show in the poem, one notes the influence of the repetition of the pronouns *nos, vos,* of the adverbs *non, bien,* and of apocopated words such as *fuert, part.* Words of three or more syllables appear in the *Cantar* in smaller proportions than they do today. Scientific, literary, and political neologisms of the modern language have increased the proportion of long words. The apocopated pronouns now pronounced as unstressed monosyllables and the multiplication of particles in the syntactic process causes this kind of words to give a smaller coefficient in the

Cantar than in contemporary Spanish. The figures corresponding to the poem appear in the following table:

Bisyllabic paroxytones	25.12%
Trisyllabic paroxytones	15.29
Stressed monosyllables	11.60
Bisyllabic oxytones	6.87
Tetrasyllabic paroxytones	2.80
Trisyllabic oxytones	1.84
Tetrasyllabic oxytones	1.00
Pentasyllabic paroxytones	0.35
Tetrasyllabic proparoxytones	0.12
Tetrasyllables with double stress	0.05
Pentasyllabic oxytones	0.05
Unstressed monosyllables	34.16
Unstressed bisyllables	0.75
	100.00

The unstressed monosyllables, articles, prepositions, conjunctions, etc., which in the individual order of the *Vocabulary* of Menéndez Pidal represent only 3.37%, go up as far as 34.16% in the composition of the text. The stressed monosyllables, *art, bien, cort, fuert*, etc. go up also from 5.62% to 11.60%; and the bisyllables, *llanos, alba, armas, campo*, etc., from 21.44% to 25.12%. Contrariwise, bisyllabic oxytones, represented for the most part in the *Vocabulary* by infinitives and singular nouns, drop from 21.73% to 6.87% upon passing through the transformations their morphology experiences in the composition of the sentences. An analogous drop is observed in the trisyllabic oxytones, from 15.61% to 1.84%, and in the tetrasyllabic paroxytones, from 6.47% to 2.80%.

The length of the sentences conforms generally to the nature of the meter.[2] Sentences that consist of exactly the two hemistichs of the verse predominate. Others, in lesser proportion, include two verses. In some cases each hemistich includes a sentence, and in other cases as many as six or eight hemistichs make up a single sentence. In the clear and sober narration of the poem it is rare for the sentences to reach greater dimensions. The first two hundred verses of the poem contain 165 sentences, among which those consisting of one hemistich number 14; of two, 116; of four, 28; of six, 4, and of eight, 3.

The essential traits of Spanish phonology already appear delineated in this ancient work in the relative frequency of the vowels and consonants as well as in the construction of the syllables, words, and sentences. In all these items, however, short lengths, established as the basic element of the language, show in the *Cantar* a greater predominance than they do today. At the time when the poem was composed, the phonological transformation had already occurred that put the *a* into first place, reduced the level of the close vowels *i, u,* increased the proportion of voiced consonants, and gave the *s* the high place it has maintained up to now. The acoustic impression of the language, founded on these proportions, must have been very similar to the one given by the language in its present state.

XIII.

Poetry and Prose

WITHIN THE PERMANENCE of its fundamental lines, the mass of phonemes of the language has not passed from one century to another without undergoing definite modifications. Such changes are not limited to the phonetic transformation of some words or to the substitution or loss of certain sounds. There exists a more general and less definable appearance in relation to the circumstances that have influenced the total aspect these materials present in the pages of each work. In the evolution of common speech, less differences have undoubtedly been produced in this sense than those that appear in literary texts.

In the verses of Gonzalo de Berceo, to judge by the result of the analysis of several stanzas of the *Vida de Santo Domingo* and of the *Milagros de Nuestra Señora*, the phonological order places the vowel *o*, as in the *Mío Cid*, immediately after the *a*, although with a slight advantage over the *e*. The frequency of these three phonemes, whose total representation rises in the stanzas referred to to 34.77%, yields individually the following figures: *a* 12.16%, *o* 11.53%, *e* 11.08%. The proportions corresponding to the other vowels are *i* 3.89%, *u* 1.56%. The monosyllabic form of the ending of the imperfects *avié*, *vinién* visibly increases the proportion of the diphthong *ie*, 2.11%. The sum of vowels and diphthongs, 48.31%, is greater in Berceo than in *Mío Cid*, 45.25%, and in both, greater than in contemporary Spanish, 43.49%.

Among the consonants, the *n* 9.25% stands out, greater than the *s* 7.61%, and more profuse than any other phoneme of this kind. One notices at first sight the repetition of words like *nin, non, nunca, omne, ninguna.* The frequency of *o* and *n*, both of a bland and obscure timbre, contributes to the grave and cordial resonance of Berceo's verses. The increase of the *o* seems to be largely the result, just as in *Mío Cid*, of the influence of the rhyme. In the *Milagros*, the most frequent rhyme is that which corresponds to the vowels *á–o*, followed, as principal types, in descending order, by *í–a, á, á–a, ó, é–o, í–o, é–a*. In lesser proportions these too are found successively: *é, ó–a, ú–a, ó–e, á–e, é–e, í, ó–o, í–e, ú–e.* Berceo utilizes in the rhymes of this work the whole repertoire of vocalic combinations, with the exception of *ú–o* and of acute *ú*.

The proportion of the phonemes in the stanzas in which Juan Ruiz describes the figure of doña Endrina places the vowels in analogous relation to what they have in the present day language. In the *serranilla* of Tablada, the open and clear sound of the *a* predominates with a proportion above the ordinary. The rhyme in *ú*, of rare and mocking effect, serves as the basis for the sullen ballad of the baker woman Cruz. The liquids *r* and *l*, raised in some passages to the highest degree among the consonants, lend assistance to the flexibility and lightness of many verses of the "Arcipreste" (Juan Ruiz). The sibilant sound of the *s*, with such a preeminent place in the language, seems checked in the *Libro de buen amor*. The agile rhythm of the *serranilla* of Tablada gives the first place, after the vowels *a, e, o*, to the suave and sonorous phoneme of *d*, which is usually found below the *s*, the *n*, and the liquids *l, r*. The *n* stands out also over the *s* in this composition. As material handled with singular intuition and dexterity, vowels and consonants, just as the combinations of rhymes and meters, show from some passages to others in this book more variation of measures than can be observed in other works.

An important modification, marked in several chapters of the *Crónica general* and the *Conde Lucanor*, consists in the increase of the level of the vowel *e*. The cause of such rise, by which this phoneme surpasses and substitutes for the *a* as the first sound of the phonological series, lies no doubt in the repeated use of the conjunction *et*, of the subjunctives *fuesse*, *oviere*, of the verbal endings corresponding to the plural of the second persons, *avedes*, *veedes*, and of the particles *el*, *me*, *le*, *te*, *se*, *que*, *de*, etc. One perceives, in effect, the sustained palatal echo of the aforementioned phoneme in the sinewy course of this ancient prose. On the other hand, in passages like "Duelo de España, in which the loose and dynamic syntax causes the diminution of the elements of grammatical relation, the *e* remains again, as it usually does, behind the *a*. On its part, the vowel *o*, strengthened by other morphological elements, presents also in these texts, as in *Mío Cid* and Berceo, a frequency index superior to what it shows in present-day language. In the order of the consonants, neither the *Crónica* nor *Lucanor* show any notable difference with respect to the figures indicated in the common scale. The standing of the voiced *s* and of the pairs *ç* and *z*, *x* and *j* is reduced to fractions as low as those indicated in reference to the poem of the Cid. The syllabic count reveals a certain excess of consonants which, in the fragments compared, gives to the checked type *bab* a visible increase over the proportion it shows in the verses of Berceo and Juan Ruiz.

The supposed cause of the preponderance of the *e* is confirmed by the fact that also in the *Corbacho* this phoneme predominates in the dissertations of a doctrinal character, where the author applies with studied style the resources proper to syntactic linking. But, on the other hand, the proportion of the *e* diminishes and the *a* recovers its superiority, with heightened standing, in the animated and clipped sentences of the imprecations of the lost hen. The *e* and the *a* come in this way to symbolize the action of the several elements that determine the difference in tone and color that exists between those passages. The preponderance of the *e* reveals the elaboration of speech under the influence of logical order. That of the *a* is a sign of an easier, more spontaneous, and more affective expression. The circumstances akin to the first have their most favorable field in prose, and those to the second are displayed mainly in verse.

In the ballad of *Abenamar*, where the proportion of the *e*,

11.34%, is considerably less than in the story of the swallows and the flax of *Conde Lucanor*, 15.52%, the *a*, on the contrary, increases to 16.26% against the 10.46% with which it figures in the aforementioned story. Against the ample and clear background of the *a*, the assonance of the rhyme of *Abenamar* underlines the tense timbre of the *i*, in intimate correspondence with the yearning attitude of the king before the beautiful Granada. The prominence the dactylic rhythm presents in most of the verses of this ballad contributes to heighten the warm temper of the composition. At the point where the king invokes the city, the transition from the even trochaic tone to the emotional dactylic accentuation has a remarkable effect.[1] Unquestionable part of the artistic harmony of *Abenamar* are the general increase of the vowel phonemes, 46.14%; the frequency of the sonorous articulation of the *r*, which in this case surpasses the dominant *s*; and the influence of free syllables, whose strengthened proportion, 67.21%, contributes to the sustained equilibrium of the verses.

In accordance with these results, the analysis of the initial paragraphs of the first chapter of *Las Moradas* of Saint Theresa assigns to the *a* the most prominent place in all the phonological material contained in them. In regard to the other sounds, the general order of the language is made manifest, with the *s* in its preferred position immediately after the *o* and with the predominance of *n*, *r*, *l* over the rest of the consonants. Something that comes out with special clarity in the aforementioned example is the concentration of the language on the three phonetic groups formed by the five vowels; by the five nasals, fricatives, and liquids, *s*, *n*, *r*, *l*, *m*; and by the original stops, *b*, *d*, *k*, *t*, *p*, *g*. The diphthongs and the rest of the palatal, fricative, and vibrant consonants appear in inferior standing, reduced at times to a minimal level.

In the first paragraphs of *Don Quijote* and *La Gitanilla*, the combination of phonemes, coinciding with the traditional lines, raises the *a* 13.85% over the *e* 11.48%; both vowels are equal, about 12.00%, in the discursive speech of the shepardess Marcela; and the *e* comes up into first place, 13.42%, as the *a* descends to 12.80%, in the elegant description of the meeting of the hero from La Mancha with the Knight of the Green Cloak. The grammatical-type phonological scheme, which in more elaborate and polished selections shows its lines by an increase in the number of coordinating particles, is attenuated in plain narration and, specially, in the passages in which Sancho converses with his master. The proportion of relatives, prepositions, and conjunctions in the serene discourses of the beautiful and discrete shepardess is considerably greater than in the animated dialogue between master and servant when Sancho gives the account of his trip to Toboso.

The study of three fragments of plays of Lope de Vega gave very similar results. The phonological notes of an intellectual and meditative character predominate. The *e* appears in the first place of the scale with a frequency average of 13.52%, while the *a* has 12.36%. The proportion of diphthongs increases, 4.31%, with examples of all the combinations used in Spanish, except *ou* and *uo*. Of the twenty-five forms of binary synalephas which the encounter of final and initial vowels gives rise to, up to twenty-two are present in these fragments, the principal ones in order of frequency being *ee, ea, oe, ae, oa, aa*. Examples of the twenty possible vowel combinations appear in the rhymes, with preference for the stressed types: *ó* 12.09%, *é* 9.15%, *á* 9.14%, *é–o* 8.49%, *á–o* 7.84%, *í* 7.84%, *é–a* 6.53%, *á–a* 6.20%, *í–o* 5.55%, *é–e* 5.55%, *í–a* 5.22%, *ó–a* 4.29%. The remaining combinations drop to small figures.[2] These cases of grammatical profusion and phonological variety are further increased with the relatively high index of syllables corresponding to the checked type *bab*, 30.18%.

On simplifying the connection of the sentences, modern literary language has reduced the phonological difference between dialectic elocution and affective expression. The vowel proportions of the prose of Azorín and of the verses of Antonio Machado coincide with the norms observed in the old writers of a clearer and plainer style. Under the constant flow of learned influences, the frequency of the voiceless stop consonants, combined often in the clusters *pt, ct*, has undergone some increase, and so has the number of checked syllables and long words. Of course, such modifications have affected the written language more than the spoken. The latter, aside from using less fully the learned vocabulary, has counteracted the relative frequency of strong sounds with the general weakening of the implosive elements of the checked syllables and with the attenuation of the expiratory intensity. The modification of the old sounds corresponding to the consonants *j*, *x*, *s*, *ç*, and *z*, must have caused very little change on the total effect of the language, considering the small role of such sounds and of those which today represent them.

The order of the vowels reflects its permanence in the predominance that definite combinations of these sounds have exercised in all times on the rhymes of verses. Among the twenty practicable types, those with the highest degree of frequency are *á–o, í–a, á–a, é–o*. It should be kept in mind that these same forms are those repeated most in the vocabulary of ordinary prose. The predominant rhymes correspond, as is logical, to the phonological conditions of the material offered with greatest frequency by the language. The relation between these rhymes with respect to the phonology of the words is similar to that which exists between the octosyllabic verse and the phonic or intonation group. The long-standing fixity in the essential traits of order and quality shown by the Spanish vowel system is no doubt responsible for the high proportion in which specially the combinations *á–o, í–a* are found, in the rhymes of Antonio Machado and Jorge Guillén as well as in the stanzas of Berceo and the assonances of the Romance ballads.

XIV.

Phonology and Pronunciation in the Rhymes of Rubén Darío

THERE SEEMS TO EXIST no indication that the voice of Rubén Darío was ever phonographically recorded. In books and articles of writers who knew him personally, there are quite abundant and detailed references on the tastes and manners of Rubén Darío. Rare, however, are the items relative to his mode of speaking.[1]

Some commentaries allude to Darío's habitual sobriety in his oral communication. At meetings and social occasions he used to keep a rather withdrawn and silent attitude. In the description given by Leopoldo Lugones of the physiognomy and character of his friend and companion, certain phrases point to the moderate tone, at once simple and distinguished, with which Darío expressed himself: "Discretion was in him like the silent suavity of velvet . . . He dressed with sober elegance and expressed himself in the same way." Speaking in another passage of the melody of Darío's verses, Lugones makes the following indirect allusion to the voice and accent of the poet: "In the peculiar accent that characterizes his voice, every man has his music."[2]

Another friend of the poet, Vargas Vila, remembered likewise the discrete and refined tone of Darío's voice and the effect one received by hearing him read his own verses: "He just finished writing and read me what he had written. His voice, lacking in resonance, without deep intonations, seemed to obey an inner rhythm, an encircling discipline that imprisoned the rhythms as in a mesh."[3] A reference to the figure that the poet presented in his last years alludes to his silent walk and his slow movements, and to the weariness that reflected in the tone and inflections of his voice.[4]

In his usual speech, Darío displayed no doubt the phonetic features peculiar to the Spanish spoken in America. The very absence of information on this point among friends and biographers indicates that in the poet's pronunciation there must have been no peculiarity that attracted attention. Aural impressions of people who still preserve the memory, now somewhat distant, of Darío's manner of speaking suggest that his diction was smooth, more slow than rapid, and more inclined to linkings and attenuation of the sounds than to articulatory reinforcement.

In the metrical treatment of words, Darío, following the traditional practice in Spanish-American poetry, observed the general norms of literary orthoëpy. These norms are the fruit of tendencies that for many generations have guided the sense of correct expression in what concerns this aspect of the language. Its social character leaves as narrow a margin to the individual's initiative as does the mechanism of grammatical morphology. Occasionally, however, Darío, turning aside from prosodic and orthographic discipline, allows certain traits of his phonological intimacy to shine through.

It is known that, although the z and the c of ce, ci are pronounced with the same sound as the s in the Spanish of America, Spanish-American poets distinguish these consonants regularly in the rhymes of their verses. The metrical tradition is a significant testimony of the permanence of the distinction between the z and the s in the orthoëpic scheme of the Spanish literary language, not only in Castile, but also in the regions of Spain where these consonants are confused. The poems of Darío have some rhymes in which the z and the c appear equated with the sound of the s.

In the section designated "Poemas de adolescencia" (1878–1881),[5] only two grooved fricative rhymes figure with intervocalic z, esa:tristeza (p. 49), desliza:brisa (p. 53), and one with word-final z, vez:ciprés (p. 48). In these same poems, the examples of regular rhyme with a distinction between intervocalic s, z, and c, rosa:hermosa, tristeza:belleza, crece:mece, amount to sixty-six, and those with a distinction of final z and s, es:pues, anís:achís, niñez:tez, cruz:luz, amount to eight. There are besides five cases of regular rhymes in which z, c, s, appear in syllable-initial position after another consonant, lontananza:esperanza, versos:diversos, and two of s before c (k), picaresca: gresca, Francisco:arisco. In these combinations the poems do not present any rhymes with the pronunciation of the c and z like s.

In "Poemas de juventud" (1881–1885), the cases of identification of the z and the c with the s between vowels amount to fourteen, sonrisa:Eloísa:hechiza (p. 115), diviniza:sacerdotisa (p. 120), empieza:espesa:francesa (p. 128), brisas:sonrisas: ceniza (p. 130), destroza:luminosa:Spinoza (p. 130), prisa: hechiza (p. 133), misterioso:sollozo:armonioso (p. 137), grandeza:progresa:naturaleza (p. 138), regazo:ocaso (p. 149), Marsellesa:entereza (p. 189), cabeza:espesa (p. 189), gozo:majestuoso (p. 211), sucia:Rusia (p. 214), amenaza:abrasa (p. 215). The examples of word-final identification of z and s are fifteen, cruz:Jesús:luz (pp. 105, 145), luz:Jesús:cruz (pp. 106, 141), voz:Dios:vos (p. 107), timidez:Moisés (p. 114), Jesús:luz (p. 117), vez:pies:brillantez (p. 123), Dios:vos:precoz (p. 142), veloz:Dios (p. 146), vez:pies (p. 165), Jerez:altivez:tres (p. 167), luz:Huss:cruz (p. 169), después:través:altivez (p. 213), compás: paz (p. 220).

Against these cases, the same "Poemas de juventud" present seventy-one examples of regular differenciation of z, c, and s between vowels and ten of analogous differentiation between word-final z and s. There is also in these poems one example of identification of z and s before a consonant, tosca:conozca (p. 160), versus three regular cases. Most of the examples of identification mentioned belong to the long poem of one hundred octosyllabic ten-line stanzas entitled "El libro." Finally, included in this same section there are twenty-six rhymes of z, c, s, pre ceded by a consonant, of the type, *esperanza:bonanza, intenso: pienso*, with no example of confusion among them.

In "El salmo de la pluma" (1883–1889), only two undifferentiated rhymes are found, *voz:Dios* (p. 245), *fisco:bizco* (p. 296). In forty-five cases of intervocalic position and in fifteen of *z, c, s* syllable-initial after a consonant, the differentiation is observed with strict regularity.

In "Epístolas y poemas" (1889), against seventy-five regular rhymes of intervocalic *z, c* and *s*, only two examples of identification appear, *melodiosos:sollozos:nemorosos* (p. 359), and *gracia:Circasia* (p. 384). Two other cases of identification are found word-final, *voz:Dios* (p. 430), *luz:Jesús* (p. 437), versus nineteen examples of regular differentiation. To this group of poems belong the only two cases of identification of *z, c, s* after a consonant recorded in the rhymes of Darío, *romance:alcance: descanse* (p. 349), *vences:pienses:dispenses* (p. 356). The first of these cases is found in a passage of a clearly humoristic nature. In another eighteen cases of this same group, the rhymes in which *z, c,* and *s* after a consonant appear are regularly differentiated. No confusion is found either in the rhymes of *s, z* plus a consonant, in which *gigantescos:pintorescos* (p. 378) and *morisca:odalisca* (p. 419), etc. occur.

Among the poems assembled in the section of "Canto épico" (1887), there is no case of *c* and *z* pronounced as *s* in the compositions of a serious tone, like those dedicated to Chile and to the Central American Union. The only two rhymes that equate *c, z* with *s* are found in the seven-syllable quatrains with alternate rhyming of "En una velada," *hechizo:paraíso* (p. 535), and in the satirical five-line stanza with which the cited section ends, *improvises:deslices:dices* (p. 550). In this same series there are eighteen regular rhymes of *z, c, s* between vowels, nine of *z, c, s* preceded by a consonant, two of *s* before *c(k)*, and eleven of *z* and *s* word-final.

Considering as a whole the preceding data, it appears that the proportion of the undifferentiated rhymes varies greatly according to the position of the consonants *z, c, s*. In the combinations in which *z, c, s* occur after another consonant, the proportion, among the seventy-five cases belonging to this type, does not exceed 2.60%. In intervocalic position, among a total of 295 examples, the proportion of undifferentiated rhymes goes up to 6.70%. In syllable-final position, before $c(k)$, the undifferentiation among the 12 cases recorded increases to 16.10%. In word-final position, among the total of seventy-seven examples, the lack of differentiation reaches as much as 24.66%.

The ratio of the 43 undifferentiated rhymes which in the totality of the 459 belonging to the poems examined make little more than 9.09%, would descend to a much lower figure if this calculation should include also the poems of *Rimas y abrojos*, *Azul*, *Prosas profanas*, and *Canto a la Argentina*, in which z, c, s appear constantly differentiated. The same goes for the books *Canto errante* and *Poema de otoño*, in which the identification of these consonants appears in entirely exceptional instances.

Darío probably pronounced the syllable-final z and s, in words like *conozca*, *picaresca*, and word-final, as in *dos*, *pies*, *voz*, *luz*, with an attenuated and weak friction that very often becomes a simple aspiration. Such sound is heard even among educated people in several provinces of the south of Spain and in the pronunciation of many Spanish Americans, specially in Central America and the West Indies. This kind of pronunciation, in which the s and the z reduce and mute their phonological individuality, seems to be the reason for the fact that in the rhymes of Darío both consonants present a greater number of undifferentiated examples when they are final than in the combinations in which their identification is checked by the normal and definite sound of syllable-initial s.

The 370 rhymes in which z, c, s appear as syllable-initial amount to more than four times the total of the eighty-nine cases in which they are found as syllable-final. Nevertheless, the examples of undifferentiation, 22 in the first case and 21 in the second, come to be equally plentiful in both positions.

These results are confirmed by the fact that the only example of undifferentiation recorded in *Cantos de vida y esperanza* (1905), belongs also to the syllable-final position, *crezcas frescas:merezcas* (p. 711). In *Poemas del otoño y otros poemas* (1910), the only two forms collected belong to the word-final position, *luz:Jesús* (p. 816), and *fugaz:jamás* (p. 846). In the section of "Baladas y canciones" there appear two other examples of this same type, *emperatriz:lis* (p. 923), *ajimez:pies* (p. 925). With these five cases, the examples of *z* and *c* equated with the *s* in the rhymes of Darío add up to forty-eight.

The evanescent and obliterated form with which the sound corresponding to the word-final *z* and *s* must have appeared in Darío's phonology had, doubtless, its most attenuated manifestation in paroxytone words. The language spoken in some regions of Spanish America and Spain reaches complete elimination of this sound. A few rhymes from the poet's youth, one of them in the seven-syllable quatrains with alternate rhyming inspired by a toast, indicate that Darío eliminated on certain occasions that weak unstressed and final sound without doing violence to his phonetic feeling, *brisas:sonrisas:ceniza* (p. 130), *ciencia:eminencias* (p. 158), *humano:manos* (p. 160), *palabra: labras* (p. 221).

In reference to the word *entonces*, it seems that Darío pronounced it without the final *s*, not for phonetic reasons nor as a poetic archaism, but because this is the usual and current form with which this word keeps its old pronunciation in the familiar speech of several countries of Spanish America—as Gagini noted in his *Diccionario de costarriqueñismos*. The measure of the verse requires in effect that the *s* with which the cited word is normally printed be omitted in the following hendecasyllables of the poem "A Víctor Hugo": "Entonce un eco de pujanza lleno" (p. 233), "Que será entonce eterna nuestra pena" (p. 233). With this same form must the said vocable be considered in the rhyme *entonce:bronce* of "Epístolas y poemas" (p. 441). At other times, under the influence of literary orthoëpy, Darío used that same word with a final *s*, *entonces: bronces* (pp. 494, 501).

It is interesting to note the coincidence of the circumstances in which the *seseo* appears in the rhymes with those in which the same phenomenon appears in some Spanish-American poets of the sixteenth century, whose verses contain the first examples of identification of z and s. The differences pointed out in Darío with respect to the proportion of the *seseo* rhymes according to the final or initial position of z and s, show a surprising similarity to the results obtained by Amado Alonso in the study of the verses of Fernán González de Eslava, who wrote in Mexico between 1567 and 1600. Already in González de Eslava, as later in Darío, the cases of lack of differentiation between z and s were found predominantly in word-final position.[6]

From the data of Fernán González de Eslava and of other writers of his time, Amado Alonso deduces that the *seseo* of the Spanish spoken in America at the end of the sixteenth century did not have the general character it now presents, but rather it must have offered a conditioned situation like the one reflected in the *seseo* rhymes of these poets. This situation, in which z and s are confused in final position while distinguished between vowels or after a consonant, is confirmed besides by the pronunciation heard at the present time in some regions of the south of Spain. In the case of Darío it can be seen, nevertheless, that the *seseo* appears also in his rhymes in a conditioned manner, although in his normal speech the author would equate entirely the pronunciation of z and c with that of the s.

The fact that the proportion of *seseo* rhymes of the type *vencen:piensen* is less than that of *grandeza:progresa* cannot be explained by the influence of his pronunciation. The situation reflected in these and in the other rhymes does not correspond precisely to the phonetic modality used by the poet but rather to the circumstances with which the differentiation of z and s must have figured in his linguistic consciousness. The images of both phonemes, maintained independently on the phonological plane, although with more assurance in some cases than in others, are reduced in usual speech to the identity of the *seseo*. It is in the field of phonology where the differentiation indicated presents a greater or lesser resistance according to the combination of the sounds and the character of the words.

The difference in proportion of the *seseo* between the rhymes of the two indicated types corresponds probably to the support the distinction of z, c, and s after a consonant must receive from the use of combinations that, on account of being less frequent, require an effort of phonological representation relatively greater than for the intervocalic *z*, *c*, and *s*. For the same reason, the proportion of identified rhymes of the type *tosca:conozca* proves to be very much lower than that of *vez:pies*, although in both forms the sound represented by the *z* and the *s*, in the general background of the *seseo*, displays similar characteristics. Among the same poems in which the oxytone rhymes with final *z* and *s* make a total of seventy-seven cases, those of *z* and *s* before *c* (*k*) do not exceed ten.

The reason why *yeísmo***** does not occur in the rhymes of Darío in similar proportion to the *seseo* must consist likewise in the relative scarcity of rhymes like *talle:valle* (p. 44), *bella:estrella* (p. 60), *arguyo:tuyo* (p. 260), *atalaya:playa* (p. 500). Certainly Darío, in his ordinary speech, did not make any more distinction between the *ll* and the *y* than between the *z* and the *s*. One can assume *yeísmo* in the pronunciation of the poet practically in all cases in which the *ll* appears in his texts. And not because of the occasional effect of limitative expression, as has been supposed in relation to certain verses,[7] but because of the ordinary habit of his mode of speaking. Nevertheless, no other example of *yeísmo* has been pointed out in Darío's rhymes than that which appears in *rayo:gallo* (p. 150) in the same composition, "El libro," that offers so many cases of *seseo* in "Poemas de juventud."

The rhymes in which sophisticated consonant clusters figure, also relatively scarce, are treated by Darío with orthoëpic regularity: *perfecto:insecto* (p. 106), *indigna:resigna* (p. 358), *acepto:concepto* (p. 360), *alumna:columna* (p. 907). Other examples show that Darío's phonology was influenced in some way by the pronunciation of these words in the classic manner, whose tradition, as it is known, remains firmly rooted in the speech of the common people, and among learned people as well in some localities. The following rhymes, in which it is necessary to disregard the consonants introduced by orthographic erudition, appear in Darío without intention of imitating the old pronun-

---

* Translator's note: the pronunciation of *ll* like *y*.

ciation: *escueto:concepto* (p. 178), *destinos:dignos* (p. 371), *columna:tribuna* (p. 371), *infinito:Egipto* (p. 444). Another rhyme that reflects the real pronunciation in spite of the cultured orthography is *istmo:abismo* (p. 900).

Of course, Darío always took into account the word-final *d*, *verdad–callad* (p. 107), *detened:sed* (p. 163). In the rhymes of two humoristic passages this sound seems to be omitted intentionally. One example is found in a hendecasyllable of *Poemas de Adolescencia*: "Señor poeta, vaya usté a paseo" (p. 65); another, in an alexandrine of *Canto errante*: "A veces me dirijo– al mercado que está–en la Plaza Mayor. ¡Qué Coppée! ¿No es verdá?" (p. 783).

The cases of lack of differentiation of *z:s*, *ll:y*, and those which present the archaic and popular pronunciation of the groups *ct, pt, gn, mn* occur, as has been seen, with very rare exceptions in the poetry corresponding to the first period of the literary work of Darío. After the publication of *Azul* (1888), not more than two or three rhymes of that kind are found in Darío's verses. Even in the works prior to this date, a large part of the examples of lack of differentiation mentioned appear in compositions of a light tone. In these, the influence of the spoken tongue shows also in expressions and turns of phrase of a familiar nature, like, "Un día que iba yo donde mi amigo," from the satirical narration "Francisco y Elisa" (p. 78), and "Que nadie se la gana en lo traviesa," from the rhymed chronicle "Tres horas en el cielo" (p. 254).

When the poet's work enters the epoch of its full artistic development, the orthoëpic abnormalities disappear from his verses. With the technical refinement of the poems of *Azul* and *Prosas profanas*, the discipline of the rhymes submits to a strict vigilance that becomes regular and permanent in the later works of Darío. But even in *Cantos de vida y esperanza* (1905), and in *Poema de otoño* (1910), his spontaneity showed itself furtively on occasion outwitting the orthoëpic principles that the poet tried to obey.

XV.

Analysis of the "Sonatina"

RUBÉN DARÍO CONSIDERED the "Sonatina" as the most harmonious of the poems contained in his book *Prosas profanas*.[1] The popularity of the "Sonatina" is based specially on the musical quality the author wished to suggest even in the very title of the composition. A phonological analysis can reveal some aspects of the delicate mechanism of this poem although it may be necessary to take apart the enchantment of his verses with calculations and statistics.

The "Sonatina" consists of forty-eight verses of fourteen syllables, distributed over eight stanzas of six verses each. The stanzas are divided in turn into semistrophes of three verses. The first two verses of each semistrophe are paroxytone and they rhyme with each other. The third is oxytone and rhymes with the third one of the respective semistrophe: *aac bbc*. Each verse consists of two hemistichs of seven syllables. The first hemistich is always paroxytone, with the exception of four that end with a proparoxytone word.

The main rhythmic supports are constituted by the last two accents of the hemistichs. Two other accents, equally regular, appear besides on syllables 3 and 10, or rather on the third of each hemistich. This type of alexandrine, to which on account of the appearance of its clauses the name of anapestic has been given, was little used by Darío. He preferred to avail himself of the iambic variety of this same verse, accented on syllables 2 and 6 of each hemistich. Many poems of Darío, like

"Los cuatro días de Elcies," "La Revolución Francesa," "Caupolicán," etc., are composed of iambic alexandrines. The anapestic alexandrine, interspersed from time to time among the iambics in some other compositions, was only employed by the poet, as a unique and uniform type, in the perfect example of the "Sonatina."

The duration of the syllables, in a moderate and current recitation of this poetry, runs through a multitude of different measures, from nine to forty-three hundredths of a second. Comparing these lengths one with another, it can be seen that there are in the verses not only long and short syllables but ultralong and infrashort ones as well. Nevertheless, such differences play only a secondary role in the verse. The syllables do not possess by themselves a quantity of their own. Their lengthening or reduction depend essentially on the accent corresponding to them and on the place they occupy in the verse.

The basic element of the rhythm consists in the regularity of the intervals between the four accentual supports each verse has. The linking intervals of hemistichs and verses, with their anacrusis and pauses, are approximately equal to the interior intervals. The structure of these verses show an intimate collaboration between syllables, quantity, and accent. The syllables, in uniform numerical series, are the raw material on which the stresses place, in conformity to a more or less strict principle of isocronism, the supports of the indicated tempos.

On these metrical patterns the verses of the "Sonatina" contain 1,570 sounds, with an average of some 34 sounds in each verse. The proportion of vowels appears in the following order: *a* 13.75%, *e* 12.87%, *o* 8.40%, *i* 4.90%, *u* 2.29%. That of the diphthongs: *ie* 0.89%, *ue* 0.57%, *io* 0.50%, *ia* 0.25%, *ai* 0.06%, *au* 0.06%, *ei* 0.06%, *iu* 0.06%, *ua* 0.06%. Missing are the diphthongs *eu, oi, ou, ui, uo,* and all the triphthongs. The total proportion of vowels, 42.22%, and that of diphthongs, 2.54%, add up to a considerably higher figure than that which results from the average of the current language, 43.49%. The increase shows specially in the most sonorous vowels, *a* and *e*.[2]

Among the consonants, the *s* appears, as always, in first place,

8.79%, followed immediately by the *l*, 8.70%, and to a some-what lower degree by the *r*, 6.62%, and the *n*, 6.62%. The soft and flexible sound of the *l* emphasizes its frequency with an extraordinary increase of 3.42% over its usual proportion. This phoneme, which in the regular scale is preceded by the *n* and the *r*, stands out in the "Sonatina" above those consonants. Besides the numerous words such as *pálida, libélula, ilusión, palacio, lago, dalias, tules,* in which the *l* appears from the beginning to the end of the poem, there are verses in which this phoneme appears with special reiteration:

> Tener alas ligeras, bajo el cielo volar.
> Ir al sol por la escala luminosa de un rayo.

There is, on the other hand, a considerable diminution in the hard and voiceless stops *p* 2.99%, *t* 2.93%, *k* 2.99%. The sum of these three phonemes is lower by more than three percent than the total with which they appear in the usual scale. The reduction affects specially the dental *t*. The other voiceless consonants, *f, ch, j, z,* with the exception of the *s,* also suffer some loss with respect to the percentages, regularly low, with which they figure in the mentioned scale.

It cannot be said that there is in the "Sonatina" a phonetic symbolism applied purposely in order to reinforce the evocative effect of the words in certain passages of the composition, but there is undoubtedly an intuitive phonological adaptation by which the musical sensitivity of the author performed with singular refinement. In spite of its relative brevity, the varied rhymes of this composition utilize up to fifteen of the twenty possible combinations. Although ordinarily Darío put great variety in the contrasts of his rhymes, the example given by the "Sonatina" on this point is not common, even in the most extensive compositions.

In the rhymes of this poem the vowels *a, o, e* predominate. These same vowels stand out likewise in the whole of the 192 rhythmic syllables of the composition. All the phonological intuition of the poet had to do in this case was to reinforce the elements that the language itself places on the most noticeable level. In this way he harmonized, along essential lines, the sonorous material of the verses of the "Sonatina" with the clear and suave background in which the fine image of the princess is portrayed: "¡Oh, visión adorada de oro, rosa y marfil!"

In this sense, the vocalic harmony that under several forms appears in many verses of the poem has a special value. By virtue of this harmony, the vowels, arranged in a special manner in accordance with their timbre, shade the unity of the verse with a kind of color rhythm. Such an effect is not here either the result of a deliberate metrical device, but rather it comes out naturally from the special aptitude of the author for expressive shading of sound. In most of the cases the said harmony refers specially to the stressed vowels:

ie-a-ue-a	Ya no quiere el palacio, ni la rueca de plata.
o-a-o-a	Ni el halcón encantado, ni el bufón escarlata.
o-a-o-a	Ir al sol por la escala luminosa de un rayo.
i-o-e-o	Y vestido de rojo piruetea el bufón.
e-o-e-u	Está presa en sus oros, está presa en sus tules.

The relation between the characteristics pointed out and the nature of the poem is evident on comparing phonologically the "Sonatina" with another composition of a different tone. In the "Responso a Verlaine" the most frequent phoneme is the *e*, 13.43%, with marked superiority over the *a*, 11.69%. The obscure vowels *o*, *u*, gain several positions in the proportional scale with the aid of somber words like *fúnebre, tumba, negrura, sombra, noche, adusto, oculto, asuste, huya, cruz*, etc. The soft *l*, represented in the "Sonatina" with an index of 8.70%, descends in the "Responso" to 5.39%. The sound of the *m*, however, with its mixed interior resonance, is raised in this latter work, and especially increased are the strong and voiceless consonants *t*, 5.30% and *k*, 4.89%. In the "Sonatina," the voiceless *p, t, k*, 8.91%, and the voiced *b, d, g*, 8.21%, appear balanced with almost equal figures, while in the "Responso" the first go up to 12.93% and the second descend to 6.79%. In short, the frequency index of the voiced phonemes, vowels, and consonants is less in the "Responso" than in the "Sonatina." Quite frequently, the rhythmic syllables in the verses of the former appear reinforced with voiceless stops:

> Que si posarse quiere sobre la tumba el cuervo.
> Y huye el tropel equino por la montaña vasta.
> Tu rostro de ultratumba bañe la luna casta.

As to the form of the syllables, the ordinary type, *ba*, rises in the "Sonatina" up to the proportion of 60.00%, with a decided advantage over the usual ratio. The type *bab*, with 28.00%, shows, too, some increase. The other combinations *a, ab, bba, bbab*, descend to proportions smaller than those which regularly correspond to them. Perhaps by a casual accident, the number of syllables shows the same amount, 82, in each one of the even stanzas, while in the odd ones, on account of the presence of final proparoxytones, there are in general 83 syllables and 85 in one single case.

The static character of the picture described by the "Sonatina" increases the proportion of the nouns, 38.00%, and lowers that of the verbs, 15.25%. The nouns, with their lordly prestige —*princesa, palacio, carroza, caballero, espada, alabardas*—and with their choice quality—*fresa, rosas, lirios, golondrina, mariposa, cisnes, lebrel, oro, diamantes, perlas, tules, mármol, marfil*—tell of the poetic foundation of the composition. Besides the repeated abstract or auxiliary forms of *ser, estar, tener, decir, querer*, etc., the verbs with specific meaning are scarce: *se desmaya, persigue, custodian, duerme, se encamina, te adora, encenderte.*

All the nouns, substantives, and adjectives, with the exception of two or three cases, occupy the places supported by the rhythmic accents. The verbs, on the other hand, on more than twenty occasions appear outside of such places, with tenuous and secondary accentuation. The second hemistich, on which the emphasis of the principal function of the rhyme falls, is the most profuse in substantives and adjectives. In the rhyme position only 5 verbs figure as opposed to 43 nouns; in the rhythmic seat immediately preceding 8 verbs are found as opposed to 39 nouns and 1 adverb; at the end of the first hemistich, a place also of outstanding prominence, the verbs are 6 as opposed to 41 nouns and 1 adverb; it is in the first rhythmic seat on the third syllable, less marked than the rest, where precisely the number of verbs goes up to 15, as opposed to 32 nouns and one adverb.[3]

The study of syllabic quantity in these same verses brings out some other things that coincide with the peculiarities just mentioned about the disposition of nouns and verbs. It shows the distribution of the expiratory accent and how, after the strong and long syllable of the rhyme, there follow in successive order the rhythmic supports of the sixth, tenth, and third syllables:[4]

El	pa la cio	so ber bio	que	vi gi lan	los	guar das
11	20 22 24	17 27 26	16	14 22 21	25	33 35

The hemistichs are distinguished in this composition by a clearly defined line, without the verbal or syntactical enjambement with which the same author joined them on other occasions. The two-part scheme of the verse is displayed in the metrical and in the grammatical order. At times each hemistich includes a sentence. More usually the hemistichs, as phonic groups with their own meaning, join and complement each other in the connection of verses and sentences. The sentence that is not limited to the single hemistich is constructed in a symmetrical manner, without odd combinations, by virtue of the sum of two, four, six, or eight hemistichs.

With the balance of the two parts of the alexandrine goes frequently the leveling of concepts rhythmically and semantically coordinated. The word situated at the end of the first hemistich corresponds to the one that occupies the end of the second: *ojos–luz, golondrina–mariposa, lirios–mayo, viento–mar, oros–tules, hipsipila–crisálida, triste–pálida*. The one that appears in the first rhythmic support is coordinated with the one that figures in the third: *suspiros–boca, alas–cielo, halcón–bufón, cisnes–lago, jaula–palacio, lebrel–dragón*. In many cases the semantic correspondence is reinforced, as can be seen, by the morphological similarity of the words.[5]

Another means of rhythmic coordination is the reiteration of identity that the poet employs often in some verses between the initial supports of each hemistich: *que ha perdido–que ha perdido, la princesa–la princesa, quiere ser–quiere ser, está presa–está presa.* At times the words corresponding to the four rhythmic stresses appear harmoniously arranged in alternating combination:

jazmines	oriente	nelumbos	norte
brillante	alba	hermoso	abril
cinto	espada	mano	azor

At other times, a change in this distribution causes the two terms of the first hemistich and the two of the second to appear in inverse order:

mudo	teclado	clave	sonoro
libélula	vaga	vaga	ilusión
occidente	dalias	rosas	sur

As is evident, the elements that contribute to give the verses of the "Sonatina" their musical character are many. It is not a question of the simple organization of the syllables of each verse under the conditions of the stress and the rhyme. The total effect comes out of the sum of the various elements: the increase and enhancement of the clearest vowels, the most sonorous consonants, and the most flexible and balanced syllabic types, the concerted impression of vowel harmony, and, finally, the influence of semantic correspondence or ideologic melody—a select and not too frequent resource considered by Darío as a superior quality of rhythm. The supports of the assigned tempos are marked with perfect regularity in many other compositions of this same poet and of other authors. But their effect does not quite produce that total harmonious impression that Darío's subtle sense of rhythm achieves in the verses of this poem.

XVI.

Gabriel Miró

AMONG THE VARIOUS aspects of the style of Gabriel Miró, the present notes try only to indicate some points in relation to the manifestations in this writer of the phonological elements of the word. For the frequency calculation of vowels and consonants the first two thousand phonemes of the chapter "El aparecido" of the novel *Nuestro Padre San Daniel* have been taken into account. The four phonemes of the first category come out in this passage with the following ratios, greater in general than those of the common scale: *a* 13.90%, *e* 12.05%, *o* 8.95%, *s* 8.77%. Those corresponding to the second group appear also for the most part heightened: *n* 7.00%, *l* 6.70%, *d* 6.55%, *r* 5.05%, *i* 4.95%. The voiceless stop of the *t* figures in Miró with 3.55%, a considerable reduction in respect to its normal rate.[1]

In the third group the ordinary frequency of the voiced phonemes, *b* 2.85%, *m* 2.45%, is maintained, while that of the voiceless ones, *k* 2.70%, *p* 2.25%, *z* 2.15% is reduced. Many of the phonemes of the fourth group, in general of infrequent use, appear in Miró with even smaller ratings than they usually present: *j* 1.00%, *ie* 0.95%, *g* 0.90%, *rr* 0.80%, *y* 0.60%, *io* 0.60%, *f* 0.40%, *ia* 0.30%, *ch* 0.25%, *ll* 0.20%, *ue* 0.15%, *ai* 0.15%, *ñ* 0.05%, *au* 0.05%, *ui* 0.05%. The palatal sounds, *y*, *ch*, *ll*, *ñ*, hardly surpass all together one percent in the fragment mentioned. The diphthongs *ei*, *oi*, *eu*, *ou*, *iu*, *ua*, *uo* are missing. The phonemes of the third and fourth groups lose nearly six percent, which is distributed among the first two categories.

A survey of these data reveals a special concentration of the phonemes that appear in the language with the greatest prominence. The preference for flexible and sonorous elements is noted specially in the diminution of sounds like *t, k, p,* which so often figure in the words with their cut off and voiceless stop. Against the background the author sets up with materials selected from common speech, unusual impressiveness results from occasional effects like the one produced in the present case by the numerous words in the fragment that reinforce the proportion of the *u: tumulto, nube, desnudo, hermosura, plenitud, maduros, quietud, profundo, anchura, nuca, luto, unto,* etc. It is rather unusual for a text of such small size to display so many nouns with this obscure vowel in the outstanding position of the stress.

The comparison of these notes with those resulting from the study of the first three paragraphs of the chapter entitled "Día campesino," from the book, *Corpus y otros cuentos,* of the same author—in which the atmosphere of a clear spring morning in the northeastern Mediterranean shores of Spain is described—offers a vivid example of the role that such effects play in the prose of Miró. The open and sonorous phoneme of *a,* which in "El aparecido" is represented by 13.90%, is raised in "Día campesino" up to 18.00%. The tense and sharp vowel *i,* recorded in the first of the said texts with a proportion of 4.95%, reaches in the second 7.00%. On the other hand, the *u* which in "El aparecido" is raised up to 3.60%, with an extraordinary increase over its regular ratio, goes down to 2.40% in "Día campesino." The sensation of light and clarity is conveyed in a few lines in this last fragment by words which for the most part contribute to that effect not only by their meaning but also by their sonority: *agua, mañana, templada, álamo, rambla, matinal, tamarindo, molino, nido, guijas, cima, centelleante, ancha, dorada, limpia, tranquila, primaveral,* etc.

For the analysis of the syllabic composition the first thousand phonetic syllables of the same chapter cited have been classified. Also apparent in this case is a considerable increase in the most common combinations at the expense of the less frequent types.

The pure syllable, of consonant and vowel, represented in the common language by 58.45%, is raised in "El aparecido" to 61.40%. The sum of this type and of that which corresponds to the scheme *bab*, goes up to 88.20%. By intuitive prosodic selection, the syllabic forms less accepted by the tradition of the language are reduced or excluded. None of these traits should lack significance in the work of a writer who, like the eager figure of the young Paulina, of Oleza, was possessed by the depth and magnificence of the sensation of things.

In the phonology of the word it is observed that Miró, following that same inclination, gives preference to the dominant patterns, raising them even more over their usual ratios. Paroxytones of two syllables account in him for 20.00% instead of 17.53%, and trisyllabic paroxytones 16.20% instead of 14.93%. The frequency index of paroxytones of four, five, and six syllables, is also greater in Miró than in the usual texts. One would say that the author searches on purpose for the effect of words of slow and smooth prosody like *terciopelo, hermosura, sensitivo*, etc. On the other hand, stressed monosyllables, which in general amount to 7.54%, do not usually reach more than 4.50% in Miró. The total proportion of paroxytones, ordinarily 38.86%, is 44.40% in Miró; that of the oxytones, regularly 10.66%, descends in Miró to 8.20%. The proparoxytones, always rare, do not surpass 2.90% in this selection. The rest, 40.00%, somewhat higher than the normal average, corresponds to the unstressed particles.

As for rhythm, the principal basis of Miro's prose is the combination of a varied series of stress groups, among which that of four syllables with stress on the next to the last one predominates. This group is followed in second place by the one of three syllables also with paroxytone stress. The groups of more than four syllables or less than three are in lesser proportions. The sum of those of three and four syllables, including words and syntagmes of both prosodic types, reaches more than fifty percent of the total. Those of four, the distinctive form of the rhythm of the language, are found sometimes in successive

series: "En su espalda—y en su nuca—se pegaba—la caliente—
devoración—de unos ojos."

The study of the phonic groups of "El aparecido" is carried
further with a count of these same units in the first chapter of
El obispo leproso. It becomes apparent that in the composition
of such groups, which are a key to the phonological construction of the sentences, the scale the author runs through does
not usually reach the extremes of brevity or amplitude that
other authors attain.

There is a marked preference in Miró for the groups from five
to nine syllables. He leans specially on those of seven, using
them with an insistence similar to that pointed out in regard
to the rhythmic groups: "Se sentía desnuda—en la naturaleza,
—y la naturaleza—la rodeaba mirándola." "Los troncos secu-
lares,—el ámbito callado—de las frondas inmóviles."

Metrified examples are found too with relative frequency
among the groups of six, eight, and eleven syllables. In the
composition of these units, it seems, the accents tend spontaneously to line up in a rhythmic order under the lyric tension
of Miró's prose. The groups conformed to such patterns combine, however, in such a way that, without failing to make their
harmony felt, hardly denote their presence in the structure of
the sentences. The few pages of "El aparecido" contain an
appreciable number of groups of six syllables in successive
disposition: "No me tenga miedo,—que yo no la sigo—más
que por su bien." "El borbollar fresco—del agua tragada." The
groups of eight syllables are likewise matched in repeated pairs:
"Avanzaba sin temer—el arrimo del labriego." "Tan dulce,
quieta y dorada—como una miel derretida." The hendecasyllables turn up from time to time with their characteristic traits:
"Todo el paisaje le latía encima." "Le despertaba un eco sensitivo." "Como rubias doncellas destrenzadas."

The author employs numerous forms in the phonological
construction of his sentences. Considering the number of groups
comprised by each unit, the 127 sentences of the chapter "El
aparecido" are distributed among sixteen distinct types. The

sentences of two groups are the most frequent; those of three occupy the second place; and those of one, the third. The sum of these three types, the shortest of the series, comprises almost seventy percent of the total. On the other hand, the sentences formed by more than five groups do not amount to one half of one percent. The brevity of the combinations recorded in this selection seems to be a dominant trait both in *Nuestro Padre San Daniel* and in *El obispo leproso*.

The ratios are different in *Figuras de la Pasión del Señor*, where the story unfolds with greater deliberation. In the chapter of "El mancebo que abandona su vestidura," from the second part of this work, the proportion of the examples of one, two and three groups, in the same number of sentences counted in "El aparecido," descends to fifty-five percent, while the long types, over five groups, increase up to twenty percent. Besides, the length of these last combinations does not go beyond seven groups in the chapter of *Nuestro Padre San Daniel*, while in the mentioned passage of *Figuras* it reaches up to fifteen of these same units. Considered in their proper dimensions, these units show also on their part a certain lengthening over the proportions given to elements of their kind in other works of Miró.

The slow and solemn effect resulting from the prolonged length of groups and sentences in *Figuras de la Pasión* is further reinforced by the expansion of the first part of the sentences. Here the author places enumerations and complementary elements before reaching the highest point of the anticadence. The contrast among the cited selections shows more or less distinctly in the comparison of other passages of the same writer. Such differences seem to arise not only from the natural relationship between the subject and the form of expression in each work, but also from the gradual turning of Miró toward that simple and refined style of which his last works are a model.

The melodic movement in the passages mentioned of *Nuestro Padre San Daniel* and *Figuras de la Pasión* displays a varied number of moderated inflections. A tense serenity pervades the narration, evoking with its intimate resonances the echo of warm and restrained emotions. No ample intervals, nor expressions of heightened prominence, nor combination of artificial musical effects come out through its reading. The elocution develops with sober harmony in which gradual transition substitutes for contrast, and suspension and circumflex modulation of the tones are more frequent than notes decidedly high or low. In this aspect, as in all others discussed, Miró purifies and colors the ordinary phonological forms, leaving on the clean lines of his style the marks of his refined sensibility.

CHAPTER I

[1] Concerning the concept of the phoneme, from Baudoin de Courtenay to Trubetzkoy, see Witold Doroszewski, "Autour du phonème," in *Travaux du Cercle Linguistique de Prague*, 1931, IV, 61–74. In the terminology of this linguistic circle the phoneme is defined as "a phonological unit that cannot be divided into smaller or simpler phonological units," *Travaux* IV, 1931, p. 315. According to the definition of N. S. Trubetzkoy, *Grundzüge der Phonologie*, Prague, 1939, p. 35, the phoneme is "the sum of the most outstanding phonological qualities of an articulated sound." Leonard Bloomfield, *Language*, 1933, p. 79, concentrating on the function that the phoneme fulfills, considers it as "a minimal unit of differentiating sound," and points out the abstract character of such a unit, remarking that phonemes are not sounds in a proper sense but models or types of sounds, p. 80. The indivisibility of the phoneme, its role as a differentiating element and its abstract nature, figure equally in the study of W. F. Twaddell, "On Defining the Phoneme," in *Language Monographs*, XVI, 1935, and in the additions of L. Novac, "Project d'une nouvelle définition du phoneme," in *Études phonologiques dédiées a la mémoire de N. S. Trubetzkoy*, Prague, 1939.

[2] The semantic function of the phoneme is highlighted in the contrast of terms that are differentiated only by one of their elements, as *peso:beso*, *cana:gana*, *poso:pozo*, *pollo:poyo*, *coto*, *codo*, *coro*, *como*, *coso*, etc.

[3] Daniel Jones proposed the term *variphone* to designate the phoneme whose variants do not come about in the systematic manner that they do in the real phoneme. Compare W. F. Twaddell, "On Defining the Phoneme" in *Language Monographs*, 1935, XVI, 26.

[4] On the relationship and differences between the two aspects of the sounds of language to which these observations refer, see Karl Bueler, "Phonetik und Phonologie," in *Travaux du Cercle Linguistique de Prague*, 1931, IV, 22–52. Amado Alonso, "La identidad del fonema," in *RFH*, 1944, VI, 280, aptly points out the character of phonology as the study of sounds in their expressive composition of signs, in contrast to phonetics,

which studies sounds in their material composition. The same Alonso has treated the modifications of Spanish phonemes with respect to their position in the syllabic group, in "Una ley fonológica del español," *Hispanic Review*, 1945, XIII, 91–101.

CHAPTER II

[1] The texts used were the first paragraphs of *Cañas y barro* of Vicente Blasco Ibáñez, *La hermana San Sulpicio* of Palacio Valdés, *El águila y la serpiente* of Martín Luis Guzmán, *Plenitud de España* of Pedro Henríquez Ureña, *Las plantas cultivadas* of Blanco Puente, *Revista Hispánica Moderna*, New York, 1942; *Revista de Historia de América*, Mexico, 1943, No. 16; *Revista de las Indias*, Bogotá, 1942, No. 41; fragments of the Madrid dailies *El Sol*, February 13, 1934; *El Debate*, February 22, 1934; *El Socialista*, March 3, 1934; and from *Excelsior*, Mexico, December 28, 1939, and *La Prensa*, Buenos Aires, February 15, 1942. The frequency of Spanish phonemes has also been studied, together with that of Italian, Portuguese, French, and Latin phonemes, by Zipf and Rogers, "Phonemes and Variphones in Four Present-day Romance Languages and Classical Latin from the Viewpoint of Dynamic Philology," in *Archives Néerlandaises de Phonétique Experimentale*, 1939, XV, 111–147. For Spanish the authors took into account 5,000 phonemes of the phonetic texts transcribed by Navarro in his *Manual de pronunciación española*, Madrid. The references made here to Italian, Portuguese, French, and Latin are based on the data of the aforementioned authors.

[2] In the count of Zipf and Rogers, the figures for these phonemes are, *a* 14.06%, *e* 12.20%, *o* 9.32%, *s* 8.12%. Within the total figures of the *e* and the *o*, the open variants have a proportion of 1.50% and 3.20% respectively. The figure for the *s* includes 0.84% corresponding to the voiced variant.

[3] The figures recorded by Zipf and Rogers for these Spanish phonemes are *n* 5.94%, *r* 5.90%, *l* 5.20%, *d* 5.06%, *t* 4.46%, *i* 4.20%. The figure for the *d* includes 3.50% for the fricative variant and 1.56% for the stop.

[4] Zipf and Rogers assign the following figures: *k* 3.84%, *m* 2.98%, *p* 2.92%, *b* 3.26%, *z* 1.74%, *u* 1.76%, *g* 1.02%. The stop variant of the *b* only represents 0.46%, included in the figure mentioned, and that of the *g*, 0.04%.

[5] The frequency index of the *f*, according to Zipf and Rogers, is in Latin 0.94%, in French 1.26%, in Italian 1.30%, in Portuguese 1.38%.

[6] Zipf and Rogers give the following figures for these phonemes: *ie* 1.06%, *rr* 1.04%, *f* 0.72%, *ll* 0.60%, *ue* 1.26%, *ia* 0.54%, *j* 0.58%, *y* 2.40%, *ñ* 0.36%, *io* 0.32%, *ch* 0.30%, *ai* 0.20%, *ei* 0.18%, *oi* 0.08%, *au* 0.18%, *eu* 0.12%, *ua* 0.06%, *iu* 0.06%, *ui* 0.54%. The proportion assigned to the *y* is probably the result of having incorporated in this phoneme some modifications of the conjunction *y*, which are conceived and employed under the phonological type of the vowel *i*, although from the phonetic point of view they coincide with that consonant.

[7] The order of frequency of the phonemes of American English has been studied, from material collected from hundreds of radio broadcasts, by Charles H. Voelker, "Technique for a phonetic frequency distribution count in formal American speech," in *Archives Néerlandaises de Phonétique Experimentale*, 1935, pp. 69–72. The results differ so greatly in respect to Spanish that, in the first three places of the scale, where Spanish has the vowels *a* 13.00%, *e* 11.75%, *o* 8.90%, English places, *i* (pip) 7.88%, *n* (nip) 7.32%, *t* (tip) 7.20%. The vowel of "pop" appears in eighth place with 4.15%, and that of "pap" in tenth, with 3.09%.

[8] It is true that the frequency of the *s* is counteracted in general by the weakness this sound undergoes in syllable-final position, a weakness which, as is well-known, precisely in the regions of the *seseo* (see translator's note on p. 19) more than in those that differentiate the *z*, becomes a simple aspiration in ordinary speech.

[9] The greater frequency of the Spanish *b* with respect to the *p* must result in part from the absorption of the *v* by the first of these consonants. For the same reason Catalan assigns the *b* 4.11%, in contrast to the *p* 2.45%, while Portuguese, which literarily distinguishes the *v*, shows for *p* 2.68% and for *b* 1.06%. With respect to *t* and *d*, the percentages in Portuguese are, according to Zipf and Rogers, 5.06% and 6.06%, but in other texts of the same language one finds respectively 5.32% and 4.11%; in Catalan, *t* 3.80%, *d* 3.68%, in Basque *p* 0.17%, *b* 4.88%, *t* 5.41%, *d* 4.17%.

[10] The count of the first 1,000 words of the lists of Milton A. Buchanan, *A Graded Spanish Word Book*, Toronto, 1927, shows the following order among the most frequent phonemes: *a* 12.24%, *r* 11.72%, *e* 11.04%, *o* 8.89%, *n* 6.35%, *i* 5.44%, *t* 5.25%, *s* 5.01%, *d* 4.24%, *k* 3.81%, *p* 3.21%, *m* 3.16%, *b* 3.03%, *l* 2.98%, *z* 2.50%, *u* 1.94%, *g* 1.44%, *rr* 1.24%, *f* 1.04%, *j* 0.97%. The large frequency of *r* is without doubt the result of the listing of the verbs under the form of their corresponding infinitives. The decline of the *s* must be produced by the absence of plurals. Dipthongs and palatal consonants appear, as usual, with minimal proportions.

[11] The total of vowels and dipthongs according to these data amount to 43.49%, and voiced and voiceless consonants, 56.51%. Zipf and Rogers assign to each of these groups, respectively, in Spanish 45.00% and 55.00%, in Italian 47.00% and 53.00%, in Portuguese 46.00% and 54.00%, and in French 44.00% and 56.00%. The authors cited note how in spite of the changes that these languages have undergone, all of them maintain approximately the same proportion of vowels and consonants as Latin, 47% and 53%. Basque shows similar figures, 44% and 56%. In English the proportion of vowels decreases and that of the consonants increases, 38% and 62%, an imbalance which is even further accentuated in German, 36% and 64%.

CHAPTER III

[1] The following pages were published in the original Spanish in the

number dedicated to the memory of Professor Ralph E. House by the journal *Philological Quarterly*, XXI, 1942.

[2] L. Rodríguez Castellano and Adela Palacio, "El habla de Cabra," in *Revista de Dialectología y Tradiciones Populares*, Madrid, 1948, IV, 387; Dámaso Alonso, A. Zamora Vicente, and María Josefa Canellada, "Vocales andaluzas," in *Nueva Revista de Filología Hispánica*, Mexico, 1950, IV, 299–330.

[3] Tomás Navarro, *El español en Puerto Rico*, Río Piedras, Editorial Universitaria, 1948, pp. 44, 46.

CHAPTER IV

[1] R. H. Stetson, the author of the most penetrating studies on the nature of the syllable, assigns to this unit first place among the phonological elements of the word (*Bases of Phonology*, Oberlin, Ohio, 1945, p. 56). Between such inseparable elements as syllables and phonemes, it is difficult to consider degrees of hierarchy. If phonemes are not produced or combined except in the nucleus of the syllable, neither can the latter on its part be conceived without the phonemes that constitute it. It is probable that consciousness of the syllable predominates in the phonetic order and consciousness of the phoneme in that of semantic differentiation.

[2] The proportions corresponding to the aforementioned consonants as phonetic syllable-finals, not counting the medial cluster relationship, are, as has been indicated previously, *-s* 4.90%, *-n* 4.11%, *-r* 1.64%, *-l* 1.59%, *-m* 0.69%. Although the words in which the syllables checked by these consonants appear belong to the general stock of the language, plain speech constantly shows a marked inclination for words formed by free syllables, as one can see by comparing the proportion in which one and the other type of syllable occur, for example, in "Abenamar" and in another ballad of a less popular character, "Don Pedro el Cruel," inserted in p. 547 of the *Romancero* of Luis Santullano, Madrid, 1937. In *Abenamar* the percentage of free syllables is 78.25%, and that of the checked ones 21.75%; in "Don Pedro," 74.35% and 25.65% respectively.

[3] The allusion here is to the sustained alliteration of imitative or humoristic character, not to certain paired expressions made up usually on a play of stop consonants, like "cal y canto," "cara o cruz," "casa y corte," "pan y palo," "polvo y paja," "tarde o temprano." J. Morawski discusses these expressions in "Les formules allitérées de la langue espagnole," *Revista de Filología Española*, 1937, XXIV, 121–163.

[4] References are found in the old treatise writers of rhetoric and poetry to this "vague and generic correspondence between the dominant sound in a clause and the nature of the thought it contains." J. Gómez Hermosilla, *Arte de hablar en prosa y verso*, Madrid, 1839, I, 374. Alfonso Reyes rightly repudiates the effort to assign immutable affective values to linguistic phonemes, and advises that the famous sonnet of Arthur Rimbaud about the vowels must be nothing but a play of wit on the part of the poet (*Tres puntos de exegética literaria*, Mexico, 1945, p. 64).

[5] Also in this case it is a question of vowel harmony of a literary character, rather than of the ablaut expressions studied by J. Morawski, "Les formules apophoniques en espagnol et roman," in *Revista de Filología Española*, 1929, XVI, 337–365.

CHAPTER VI

[1] The studies published by the author on the quantity of sounds in Spanish pronunciation in *Revista de Filología Española*, Madrid: "Cantidad de las vocales acentuadas," 1916, III, 387–408; "Cantidad de las vocales inacentuadas," 1917, IV, 371–388; "Diferencias de duración entre las consonantes españolas," 1918, V, 367–393; "Historia de algunas opiniones sobre la cantidad silábica española," 1921, VIII, 30–57; "La cantidad silábica en unos versos de Rubén Darío," 1922, IX, 1–29, can serve as a point of comparison.

[2] In French and Italian the contrast between long and short syllables seems even greater than in Spanish. Syllables greater than 50 hundredths of a second next to others extremely short were noted in the reading of some verses of Victor Hugo, by M. Grammont, *Les vers français*, Paris, 1913, pp. 88–89. Analogous extremes appear in the recording of some verses of Manzoni measured by Panconcelli-Calzia, "Experimentalphonetische Untersuchungen über den italienischen zehnsilbigen Vers," in *Med. päd. Monatschrift für die ges. Sprachheilkunde*, Berlin, XVIII, 1908.

CHAPTER VII

[1] The author has dealt with this theme, without special reference to the phonological aspect, in "Palabras sin acento," *Revista de Filología Española*, 1925, XII, 335–375.

CHAPTER IX

[1] Omitted in this chapter are some illustrative charts. Instead new data have been added that were not included in its first edition, which appeared with the title of "El grupo fónico como unidad melódica," *Revista de Filología Hispánica*, 1939, I, 3–19.

[2] The name of rhythmic-semantic group, used by M. Grammont and repeated by me on other occasions, is more adequately applicable to designate the stress group as a constituent part of verse.

[3] H. Klinghardt, "Sprechmelodie und Sprechtakt," in *Die Neueren Sprachen*, 1923, XXXI, 1–29.

[4] The preponderance of sentences of seven, eight, and nine syllables in the composition of Spanish prose has been noted specially, heretofore, by R. Brenes-Mesén, "El ritmo de la prosa española," in *Hispania*, 1938, XXI, 47–52.

[5] R. Menéndez Pidal, *Cantar de Mío Cid*, Madrid, 1908, I, 99–103, and "Roncesvalles," in *Revista de Filogía Española*, 1917, IV, 128–138.

[6] "An Analysis of Reports of Physical Examination from 21 Selected States," in *Medical Statistics Bulletin*, Washington, D. C., 1943, No. 2, tables 7 and 8.

CHAPTER X

[1] These observations amplify the data anticipated on this material by Tomás Navarro, *Manual de entonación española*, New York, 1945, pp. 54–59. As regards the general theory of the structure of the sentence from the phonological point of view, see Serge Karcevskij, "Sur la phonologie de la phrase," in *Travaux du Cercle Linguistique de Prague*, 1931, IV, 188–227.

CHAPTER XI

[1] We have made several additions to this study which first appeared in Madrid in 1935.

[2] Maestro Barbieri, in his discourse on "La música de la lengua española," published in *La España Moderna*, IV, no. 40, 1892, did not refer precisely to accent; he simply wrote about certain principles of acoustics common to music and language, and some forms of intonation of an equally general nature. Previously, Sinibaldo de Más, in *Sistema musical de la lengua castellana*, in his *Obras literarias*, Madrid, 1852, was not concerned either with accent, but limited himself to expounding his artificial theory concerning syllabic quantity.

[3] A. de Eximeno, *Del origen y reglas de la música*, Madrid, 1796, III, 165 ff.

[4] E. Buceta, in a documented article on "El juicio de Carlos V acerca del español y otros pareceres sobre las lenguas romances," in *Revista de Filología Española*, 1937, XXIV, 11–23, proved that this opinion, with slight variations, is mentioned by Girolamo Fabrici d'Acquapendente, 1601; by Jacques David, Cardinal du Perron, 1556–1618; by Nicolás Mulmen, a German, 1618, and by the Frenchman, P. Bouhours, 1628–1702, which shows that the saying of the emperor was known in several countries long before the date when Mayans and Forner mentioned it. The phrase very probably was not authentic, but inspired by such famous events as the discourse of Charles V, in Spanish, before Pope Paul III, 1536. The nature and meaning of this expression make it difficult to believe that it entered Spain by way of Bouhours, or that it could have arisen in any land except the Peninsula, where perhaps it circulated as an oral anecdote, before appearing in foreign or Spanish books.

[5] Juan de Iriarte, "Epigramas," in *Biblioteca de Autores españoles*, LXVII, 498.

[6] Madame de Staël, *De l'Allemagne*, Paris, Didot, 1845, p. 135.

[7] The praises of this kind which speak with the greatest eloquence about the qualities of Spanish are those of Fernando de Herrera, *Anotaciones a Garcilaso*, Sevilla, 1580; Bernardo de Aldrete, *Del origen y principio de la lengua castellana*, Roma, 1606; Juan Pablo Forner, *Exequias de la lengua castellana*, 1782, and Emilio Castelar, *Discurso de ingreso en la Academia Española*, in *Memorias de la Academia*, vol. VI, Madrid, 1889.

[8] The brilliant synthesis with which Alfonso Reyes begins his "Discurso por la lengua," in his book *Tentativas y orientaciones*, Mexico, 1944, pp. 197 ff, is distinguished among the more recent judgments of Spanish American writers by the accuracy and sense of its observations.

[9] Juan Bautista Alberdi, *Autobiografía*, Buenos Aires, 1927, p. 64.

[10] Domingo F. Sarmiento, *El premio de lectura*, in *Obras completas*, VLI, 201.

[11] E. S. Zeballos, "El castellano en América," prologue to *Notas al castellano en la Argentina* of Monner y Sans, Buenos Aires, 1924, p. 10.

[12] Review of *Ancient Spanish Ballads* of Lockhart in *The Edinburgh Review*, 1841, LXXII, 403.

[13] Hillard's text is found in E. Buceta, "La tendencia a identificar el español con el latín," in *Homenaje a Menéndez Pidal*, I, 103, n.

[14] F. Wulff, "Un capitre de phonétique," in *Recueil de mémoires philologiques présenté à Gaston Paris*, Stockholm, 1889, p. 216.

[15] G. Borrow, *La Biblia en España*, translation of M. Azaña, Madrid, I, 53.

[16] R. Menéndez Pidal, Prologue to *A Primer of Spanish Pronunciation*, T. Navarro Tomás and Aurelio M. Espinosa, New York, 1926.

[17] Miguel Antonio Caro, *Manual de elocución*, in Obras completas, V, 292.

[18] For Casanova's opinions on Spanish, see Jean Sarrailh, "La sonorité de la langue espagnole," in *Revista de Filología Española*, 1935, XXII, 285–286.

[19] Edgar Quinet, *Mis vacaciones en España*, Madrid, 1931, p. 41.

[20] Waldo Frank, *España virgen*, Madrid, 1927, pp. 216–218.

[21] L. Malefille, "Étude du caractère de la langue espagnole," in *Cours de langue espagnole*, Paris, 1854. The same opinion is given by H. Gavel, *Essai sur l'évolution de la pronunciation du castillan*, Biarritz, 1920, p. 511.

[22] S. de Madariaga, *Ingleses, franceses y españoles*, Madrid, 1929, p. 309.

[23] *Oeuvres complètes de Branthôme*, ed. Bibliothèque Elzevirienne, IX, 79.

[24] Benito Feijoo, "Paralelo de las lenguas castellana y francesa," in *Teatro crítico*, ed. A. Millares, Madrid, La Lectura, I, 269.

[25] J. F. Pastor, *Las apologías de la lengua castellana*, Madrid, 1929, p. XIX.

[26] W. R. Shepherd, of Columbia University, ap. E. C. Hills, in *Hispania*, California, 1923, VI, 146, n.

[27] J. B. Trend, *A Picture of Modern Spain*, London, 1921, p. 85.

[28] L. P. Thomas, *Le lyrisme et la préciosité cultiste en Espagne*, Halle, 1909, p. 22.

[29] G. Zaldumbide, *Significado de España en América*, New York, 1933, p. 32.

[30] J. Storm, "Romanische Quantität," in *Phonetische Studien*, 1889, II, 147.

[31] J. Storm, *Englische Philologie*, Leipzig, 1892, II, 186–187.

[32] Ap. M. Romera Navarro, *El hispanismo en Norteamérica*, Madrid, 1917, p. 56.

[33] L. Díaz, "A la lengua española," in *Programa de lengua española*, of C. Gómez Tejera, San Juan, Puerto Rico, 1933, p. 460.

[34] J. P. Forner, *Exequias de la lengua castellana*, Madrid, La Lectura, 1925, p. 91.

[35] F. A. Barbieri, "La música de la lengua española," in *La España Moderna*, 1892, IV, No. 40, p. 157.

[36] W. von Schlegel, *Sämtliche Werke*, XI, 419, ap. J. J. A. Bertrand, *Cervantes et le romantisme allemand*, Paris, 1914, p. 135.

[37] Edgar Quinet, *Mis vacaciones en España*, Madrid, 1931, p. 61.

[38] W. Somerset Maugham, *Of Human Bondage*, New York, 1940, p. 474.

[39] F. Wulff, "Un chapitre de phonétique," in *Recueil, présenté à Gaston Paris*, Stockholm, 1889, p. 216.

[40] Cervantes, *Teatro*, ed. Schevill y Bonilla, III, 218.

[41] J. Benavente, *Teatro*, Madrid, 1913, I, 25.

[42] "My lord baron!," exclaimed the priest with the emphatic tone of a ham actor, "your soul is as ugly as your face!," A. Palacio Valdés, *El Maestrante*, Madrid, 1915, p. 344.

[43] I. Gil Reglero, *Limba spaniola. Gramática española para rumanos*, Bucarest, 1934.

[44] G. Mayáns y Siscar, *Orígenes de la lengua española*, Madrid, 1737, I, 195.

[45] A. de Capmany, *Filosofía de la elocuencia*, Madrid, 1777, p. 32.

[46] Academia Española, *Gramática de la lengua castellana*, Madrid, 1928, p. 511.

[47] J. B. Trend, *A Picture of Modern Spain*, London, 1921, p. 85.

[48] Cristóbal Suárez de Figueroa, *El pasajero*, ed. Bibliófilos Españoles, Madrid, 1914, XXXVIII, 418.

[49] F. Navarro Ledesma, "Égloga," en *Prosistas Modernos*, ed. de Díez Canedo, en la Biblioteca del Estudiante, Madrid, 1922, p. 252.

[50] A. de Eximeno, *Del origen y reglas de la música*, Madrid, 1796, III, 176.

[51] R. del Valle Inclán, *La lámpara maravillosa*, Opera Omnia, Madrid, 1916, I, 77.

[52] P. Henríquez Ureña, "El supuesto andalucismo de América," in *Cursos y conferencias*, 1936, X, 818.

[53] Amado Nervo, in "Cómo se habla el español en España," after pointing out the deep tone and the harshness of the *j* in the Castilian pronunciation, alludes to his country's accent: "our relatively high pitch, our

frequently metallic timbre, the softness of our inflections at times excessive." *Obras completas*, 1921, XXII, 137. P. Henríquez Ureña points out the lack of vigor in the emission of sounds, the slow tempo, the high tone, the winding and connected phonic current, the close timbre of the vowels and the tense and precise articulation of the consonants as the principal features of the Spanish of the high plateau of Mexico: *El español en México, los Estados Unidos y la América Central*, Buenos Aires, 1938, p. 335.

[54] O. Rutz, *Musik, Wort und Körper als Gemütsausdruk*, Leipzig, 1911, p. 229, and *Vom Ausdruk des Menschen*, Celle, 1925, p. 46 ff.

[55] Eça de Queiroz, *A Correspondencia de Fradique Mendes*, ap. R, Landa, "La enseñanza de las lenguas vivas," in *Boletín de la Institución Libre de Enseñanza*, Madrid, 1926, L, 40.

[56] Ch. Bally, *Traité de stylistique française*, Heidelberg, 1911, I, 54.

[57] R. Menéndez Pidal, *Orígenes del español*, Madrid, 1926, I, 503 and 514.

[58] Hernando del Pulgar, *Claros varones de Castilla*, ed. J. Domínguez Bordona, Madrid, La Lectura, 1924, pp. 32, 40, 60, 163.

[59] R. Menéndez Pidal, "El lenguaje del siglo XVI," in *Cruz y Raya*, 1933, No. 6, p. 27.

[60] E. Sievers, *Rhythmisch-melodische Studien*, Heidelberg, 1912, pp. 78–111.

[61] The investigation technique applicable to this subject can be seen in G. Ipsen and F. Karg, *Schallanalytische Versuche*, Heidelberg, 1928.

[62] M. Weingart, "Étude du langage suivi du point de vue musical," in *Travaux du Cercle Linguistique de Prague*, 1929, I, 181–182.

[63] R. Menéndez Pidal, "Sobre las vocales ibéricas *e* y *o* en los nombres toponímicos," in *Revista de Filología Española*, 1918, V, 225 ff.

[64] J. Saroïhandy, "Vestiges de phonétique ibérienne en territoire roman," in *Revista Internacional de Estudios Vascos*, 1913, VII, 475–497.

[65] T. Navarro Tomás, Aurelio M. Espinosa (son), and L. Rodríquez Castellano, "La frontera del andaluz," in *Revista de Filología Española*, 1933, XX, 262 ff.

CHAPTER XII

[1] R. Menéndez Pidal, *Cantar de Mío Cid*, Madrid, 1908, I, 113–120.

[2] We have pointed out previously, page 72, the merely automatic character of the alternating decrease in the proportion of long and short hemistichs, coinciding with the length of the phonic groups and of other phenomena of a fluctuating nature, pages 72–74.

CHAPTER XIII

[1] These notes are completed by some references from the commentary to the ballad of "Abenamar" written by Leo Spitzer in the review *Asomante*, San Juan, Puerto Rico, 1945, I, 7–20.

[2] In the plays of Lope, the assonances of the 1,656 passages versified in the form of ballads, according to the tables of S. Griswold Morley and Courtney Bruerton, *The Chronology of Lope de Vega's Comedias*, New York, 1940, pp. 394–402, appear in the following order of frequency: *é–a* 20.16%, *é–o* 19.50%, *á–a* 17.99%, *á–o* 8.33%, *á–e* 6.34%, *í–o* 5.61%, *é–e* 4.59%, *ó–a* 3.86%, *í–a* 3.56%, *o–o* 1.93%, *í–e* 1.81%, *ó* 1.57%, *ó–e* 1.57%, *í* 0.72%, *ú–o* 0.66%, *á* 0.60%, *é* 0.60%, *ú–a* 0.30%, *ú–e* 0.24%. Among the assonances predominant in the *Romancero* of Durán only *á–a* is also abundant in the ballads of Lope. The forms *á–o*, *í–a*, which in the ballads immediately follow the type *á–a*, are found in Lope in fourth and ninth place. The first two combinations of the ballads of Lope, *é–a*, *é–o*, are found on the other hand in fourth and sixth places in the old ballads. The fragments examined of "La corona merecida," "Pedro Carbonero" and "El marqués de las Navas," all of them in *redondillas* (eight-syllable quatrains with rhyme abba or abab), coincide in emphasizing acute rhymes, notwithstanding the differences of date between the first two plays, 1603, and the third, 1624. But the aforementioned fragments are not sufficiently extensive to represent the tendencies which may exist in the immense field of Lope's consonants. The rhymes in *é–a*, *é–o* are the predominant types in the calculation of several hundreds of *coplas* (verses) of the *Cantos populares* of Rodríguez Marín, Sevilla, 1892, of 740 verses of Bécquer, 2,420 of Valle Inclán, and 3,174 of Juan Ramón Jiménez. The frequency of *e–o*, produces in careless prose homophonies like that of the following passage: "Para andar marchaba apoyado en un bastón *grueso*, dando golpes en el *suelo*, como un *ciego*." Baroja, *Los recursos de la astucia*, Chapter III.

CHAPTER XIV

[1] Several modifications have been made in this chapter, which appeared originally with the title "La pronunciación de Rubén Darío," in the *Revista Hispánica Moderna*, New York, X, 1944.

[2] L. Lugones, "Rubén Darío," in *Ediciones selectas América*, Buenos Aires, 1919, I, 272–273.

[3] Vargas Vila, *Rubén Darío*, Madrid, 1917, p. 46.

[4] R. Cansinos-Asséns, "Un recuerdo," in *La ofrenda de España*, by J. González Olmedilla, Madrid, 1916, p. 52.

[5] The pages cited refer to the edition of *Obras de Rubén Darío* compiled by Alberto Ghiraldo, Madrid, M. Aguilar, 1937.

[6] Amado Alonso, "La pronunciación americana de la z y de la c en el siglo XVI," in *Universidad de la Habana*, 1939, IV, No. 23, and "Biografía de Fernán González de Eslava," in *Revista de Filología Hispánica*, 1940, II, 266–268.

[7] A. Coester, "The Influence of Pronunciation in Rubén Darío's Verse," in *Hispania*, California, 1932, XV, 258.

CHAPTER XV

[1] Rubén Darío, *Historia de mis libros*, Madrid, Yagüe, 1919, p. 190.

[2] Vowels in synalepha have been counted as independent phonemes when they are distinct, *ae, eo*, and as a single vowel they are identical and form a single syllable: "se escapan," "sobre el trueno."

[3] The correspondence between phonological and semantic lines, although it rarely attains such perfect symmetry as in the present example, is characteristic of the nature of poetry in all languages. See Jan Mukarowsky, "Rapports de la ligne phonique avec l'ordre des mots dans les vers tchèques," in *Travaux du Cercle Linguistique de Prague*, 1929, I, 121–139, and "La phonologie et la poétique," in the same journal, 1932, IV, 278–288.

[4] The study of the Sonatina as to the quantitative relation of its syllables can be seen in Tomás Navarro, "La cantidad silábica en unos versos de Rubén Darío," in *Revista de Filología Española*, 1922, IX, 1–29.

[5] Dámaso Alonso in "Temas gongorinos," *Revista de Filología Española*, 1927, XIV, pointed out similar cases of verbal symmetry in Góngora's hendecasyllables.

CHAPTER XVI

[1] The edition used here is *Obras Completas de Gabriel Miró*, Madrid, Biblioteca Nueva, 1943.

Index